The Silv
Spe

THE CHRISTMAS BOX

By Paul Magrs

Published December 2017 by Obverse Books
Cover Design © Cody Schell
Text © Paul Magrs

Range editor: Stuart Douglas

2018 Titles

Contents

Introduction

It's a strange thing when Christmas suddenly gets cancelled and the whole festive world starts to fade away. All the tinsel and glitter pales and everyone around you seems to be acting completely mad. You wonder: what are people *doing* all day? Surrounded by shiny new junk and shredded wrapping paper, eating as much as they possibly can, forcing jolliness on each other and scorching out their eyeballs with as much telly-watching as they can possibly manage?

Even in my alienated state I knew that these were wonderful things to do at Christmas, and I'd have given anything to rejoin the human race and do all the stuff I'd done every Christmas Day of my life so far. But, as it was, 2015 was different. It was horrible.

My partner Jeremy was in hospital. It had happened on Christmas Eve, in the very early hours. We had spent the evening of the twenty-third happily starting up the festivities with a first night's worth of vintage Christmas Telly and then, in the very early hours his Crohn's disease flared up for the first time in nineteen years and I had to call an ambulance.

It's a strange feeling. A disaster movie happening in a small, localised spot. Sitting inside a bright ambulance right outside your own house in the middle of the night. All the neighbours are sleeping and all the lights stay dark and no one is aware of the drama going on within. No one else knows about the painkillers swiftly administered, the phone calls made, the stricken wordless glances and the feeling that your lives have been taken out of your hands and that everything is in someone else's control right now.

That feeling persisted all the way to Manchester's Royal Infirmary and our progress through waiting rooms and cubicles, room after room, question after question, proddings and pokings and forms and more questions. We met porters and nurses and doctors and surgeons. Jeremy answering the same questions from all of them, wincing and crying out in pain and, eventually, some time after dawn, getting wheeled onto a ward. We both dozed a little at about 10 am. This shared ward was full of noisy old men. One of them had large headphones clamped to his head, singing along tunelessly with Frank Sinatra, guessing at the words. '*I picked myself up and put myself back into the race... and that... that's whatchacallit... That's life...!*'

I nipped out in the late afternoon. I walked home on Christmas Eve, hurrying through the chilly South Manchester streets, just as the brief daylight was fading. The traffic was shunting slowly along, taking everyone home for Christmas. The lights of homes in Victoria Park, Fallowfield and Levenshulme were glowing with lit-up trees. Our own decorations weren't yet up and they wouldn't be going up any time soon. I was dashing back to fetch pyjamas and a wash bag and anything else I thought he might need. I was repeating inside my head all the things I'd need to remember as I hurried along the old Victorian streets.

I was anticipating at least a week of going back and forth between home and hospital wards as they struggled to get his crazy insides under control, and decided whether he'd need surgery or not. By teatime on Christmas Eve we knew he'd never be home for Christmas. They'd pumped him full of intravenous steroids, hoping to shrink the inflammation of his bowel, and he'd be stuck there for days. The fleeting fantasy that he'd be sent home on Christmas Eve – just in time – and told only to drink weak tea and custard evaporated with the daylight. He was on a seventy-two hour drip and he needed careful eyes on him. One way or another, our Christmas was cancelled.

As I hurried towards our street by the railway lines in Levenshulme, I was worried about our cat, Bernard Socks. In the early hours of last night he hadn't been around. He slept much of the night on our bed, usually, with a few forays out in the night garden via the catflap. I hadn't seen him since we set off in the ambulance and so he hadn't been fed all day. I was hoping fiercely that he'd been okay in our absence and then, as I turned the corner onto Chestnut Avenue, there he was! And it was the strangest thing. At first I thought I was hallucinating because of sleep deprivation. But he was dancing down the middle of the road. On his hind legs. Skipping towards me.

The weirdness of his apparently psychic timing and the fact of his dancing like Puss-in-Boots on Christmas Eve passed me by in a blur of happy tiredness and relief that he was okay. He dashed indoors with me, eager for food and treats. I had bags to pack, phone calls to make and the pilot light on the boiler to fix. (My first go at a shower and the water was freezing!)

Then I flopped down in front of the telly.

I made the phone calls I had to – family, friends and neighbours, telling them what had happened.

And on the telly there was something brand new.

A piece of Christmas Telly that was so perfect and unexpected that it even managed to calm me down for a few minutes. It soothed me. It stole away the feverish and exhausted panic of Christmas Eve 2015.

Bernard Socks came slouching in and hopped up onto my knee and we watched these Laplanders, their sleighs and some reindeer contentedly traversing a snowy landscape that was lilac and delicately crunchy. Hours and hours passed. They muttered a few words to each other. They called out hellos to the occasional friends they happened past. The sky darkened. Sleigh bells tinkled. The snow crunched and crumped.

This was all that happened during this very subdued odyssey and it was bliss. It was the very opposite of the noisy glitz and razzamatazz that you might expect to enjoy on Christmas Eve telly.

The uneventfulness suited me just fine.

I knew right away that **All Aboard! The Sleigh Ride** on BBC 4 was going to be a new addition to my little collection of Christmas Telly.

I have a box of Christmas Telly. A true Box of Delights. It's a carefully curated batch of discs and tapes that has taken me a lifetime to accrue. It's eccentric but wonderful. It's what I'd be watching on a Christmas Desert Island.

That dreadful Christmas of 2015 I spent every evening alone in our house. The hours when I wasn't visiting Jeremy in the hospital I was at home alone, re-watching all my favourite Christmas Telly.

These aren't just bits of daft nostalgia or camp classics or vintage gold. These are life-sustaining things.

I watched them all again, night after night until New Year, thinking of better Christmases in the past, and hopefully jollier ones to come.

Blankety Blank

Episode Title: Christmas

Channel: BBC 1

Original UK Transmission Date: 26 December 1981

Regular Cast: Terry Wogan (Presenter)

Guest Cast: Beryl Reid, Larry Grayson, Lenny Henry, Jimmy Tarbuck, Liza Goddard, Lorraine Chase

A game show in which contestants attempt to come up with plausible alternatives to missing words in a supplied phrase, and hope that one or more of the celebrity panel agrees with them.

A cheap and cheerful show I adored, and here it's the interplay between the celebrity guests that makes the show sparkle. Beryl Reid and Larry Grayson sit side by side, giggling and carrying on. Has there ever been a greater collision in the history of on-screen camp? Shouldn't the universe end in a shattering explosion and a rift open up in the time-space continuum because of the nearness of these two icons of silly innuendo?

Larry and Beryl barely have to say a word to be funny. They just have to give the slightest look. In the same edition, Jimmy Tarbuck and Lenny Henry are working hard as they can (slightly too hard, actually) to get the laughs. Larry and Beryl aren't exactly restrained, but they know just how to bring down the house with the smallest of moues at the camera and a 'Shut it, you.' Larry always looks like someone's raw-boned maiden aunt in mannish drag; Beryl is a tiny, elegant thing, with immaculate whiskers, flashing eyes and concealed claws. You can smell the gin coming off the screen in waves.

I remember watching this episode quite clearly, at the age of twelve. I even wrote in my diary how hilarious it was that Terry Wogan had said, 'It's quite exciting, this game,' and Beryl replied: 'I'm finding it knicker-gripping.' At the age of twelve I thought that was about the funniest thing I had ever heard. She's querulous, rude and droll, all at the same time.

Wogan prods and cajoles his guests, with that ridiculous wand of a microphone. They all gently send up the contestants – including the slightly odd, forbidding Edith. She wins – not the video recorder or the music centre – but the wooden backgammon set. This was a somewhat duff prize, even back in 1981. Edith announces that she can't even play backgammon, but she's quite good at Ludo. When the next contestant, Elizabeth, wins the very same thing, Terry tells them they will have to fight each other for it.

I love the easy questions, the daft rude jokes, the fake bickering and the determined naffness of it all. When I was a kid I used to imagine how, following the recording of **Blankety Blank**, the contestants and the celebrity guests would all go off to the BBC bar at TV Centre and get happily trashed together, mingling queasily with the other stars: Basil Brush and the Wombles, the Two Ronnies, Pan's People and Doctor Who. The noise of the theme tune and the studio audience applause would still be ringing in their ears. They'd be clutching their souvenir silver cheque books and pens and the victor would be holding onto her leatherette backgammon set for dear life.

The Box of Delights

Episode Titles: When the Wolves Were Running... (1 November 1984)

Where Shall the 'Nighted Showman Go? (8 November 1984)

In the Darkest Cellars Underneath (15 November 1984)

The Spider in the Web (22 November 1984)

Beware of Yesterday (29 November 1984)

Leave Us Not Little... Nor Yet Dark (6 December 1984)

Channel: BBC 1

Original UK Transmission Dates: 1 November – 6 December 1984

Regular Cast: Devin Stanfield (Kay Harker), Robert Stephens (Abner Brown), Patrick Troughton (Cole Hawlings)

Main Guest Cast: Geoffrey Larder (Foxy Faced Charles), Jonathan Stephens (Chubby Joe), Heidi Burton (Jemima), Joanna Dukes (Maria), Flora Page (Susan), James Grout (Inspector), Carol Frazer (Caroline Louisa), Crispin Mair (Peter), Glyn Baker (Herne the Hunter), Patricia Quinn (Sylvia Daisy Pouncer), John Horsley (Bishop of Tatchester), Charles Pemberton (Chief Constable)

Writer: Alan Seymour, adapted from John Masefield

Director: Renny Rye

On a visit to stay with relations over the holidays, Kay Harker encounters an old Punch and Judy man and finds himself drawn into a world of magic and peril.

I was a kid who'd grown up with BBC adaptations of children's classics. I watched with my mam. All these books that would have been too girly (apparently) to borrow from the library. **The Secret Garden, The Enchanted Castle, Carrie's War**. By 1984 I was fifteen and, really, I ought to have grown out of children's books and TV – and that included **Doctor Who**. I was choosing my O-Level subjects and it was time to think about grown-up stuff.

But Christmas 1984 brought a surprising extra gift: the kind that lasts a lifetime. It was a TV serial based on a book I had never heard of. And, with six episodes broadcast between my birthday and Christmas Eve, this serial ensured that I never quite grew out of kids' TV, kids' books, Christmas, or magic, my entire life. I will always be grateful to **The Box of Delights** for that. I feel like they somehow parcelled up the very essence of Christmas in this production and preserved it well-nigh perfectly.

I was drawn into this mysterious package... by what, exactly?

Mostly, beautifully-evoked nostalgia for an era I never grew up in. We visit a 1930s of steam trains and quaint snowy towns where it seems mysteries and adventures are absolutely obligatory, especially during the festive season. The arch campery and daft lingo of public schoolboys, dotty aunts and sinister clerics burble pleasantly throughout, along with a soundtrack that's a perfect mélange of Victor Hely-Hutchinson and Roger Limb of the Radiophonic Workshop.

The Box of Delights also has the most terrifying title sequence and spooky title theme TV has ever produced.

And then we have the wonderfully warm appearance of a shabby, bearded Patrick Troughton, stomping down the station platform with his Barney Dog: a travelling showman who claims he dates back to Pagan times. He twinkles and grimaces and warns our young hero Kay to watch out for the wolves. 'The wolves are running,' he purrs darkly, and I can feel those shivers going up my spine, typing that line even in the middle of a red hot July.

It was like tuning into a Christmassy **Doctor Who** story that someone had accidentally written fifty years too early. A story steeped in the magic and folklore of bygone times, and set in the golden years between world wars. This first viewing was a lesson to me that the magical essence I found irresistible in **Doctor Who** actually existed outside of that blessed series. It is in fact a form of genre-blending story-telling that is also present in earlier tales: of Narnia, Sherlock Holmes, Mary Poppins, HG Wells, Kenneth Grahame, Edith Nesbit, Lewis Carroll. It's all a form of British fantasy and whimsy, and this 1984 adaptation of Masefield was a Pandora's Box containing elements of all these favourite things. It actually weaned me off an exclusive love for **Who** and drew me into literary fantasy and folklore, and for that I'll always be grateful.

Grateful, also, for so many other moments. For packing breakfast feasts in the pantry at dawn, swiping sausage rolls and jam tarts and taking them into the snowy wilds with your best pal and observing flying motorcars and distant scrobblings. Grateful for Maria Jones and her pistols and hankering for gangsters. Grateful for the best villain in the world: Robert Stephens being the epitome of sophisticated cruelty and avarice, while Patricia Quinn as his delectable Daisy Pouncer almost steals the whole show. She's the girl with the maniacal cackle in her voice.

Grateful, also, for: 'Now, be a stag in the wild wood with me!' Oh, that very moment when Kay gets to journey inside the Box itself, and it opens out into woodlands and Herne the Hunter is there and he looks just like the lead singer of some New Romantic band. They run together, becoming stags and birds and fish, all in a flurry of wishy-washy water colour animation.

All these delicious visuals were state of the art in 1984. People might point and laugh at some of the creaking, fuzzy effects now, but this was all breathtaking then. They threw every kind of visual effect they could muster at the screen for this show: theatrical and costume effects, electronic and fledgling computer effects, beautifully drawn animation. Every frame of it glimmers with ingenuity and brilliance. It's a proud hotch-potch of styles, looking sometimes like a video for a pop group of the time. There's just as much Human League as Lancelyn-Green about this children's classic. The bewildering patchwork of styles works stunningly. I remember the wonderful feeling, as a kid watching this, that you had absolutely no idea where the next episode might take us. The pic-n-mix quality of styles matches the heterogeneity of John Masefield's influences: his novel veers and darts between alchemists, ancient Greeks, and Punch and Judy.

And, even though there's always a slight disappointment that Troughton's utterly captivating Cole Hawlings only really appears in half the episodes, his return at the end is a triumph. He's a kind of Woolworths Gandalf, cheerfully cut price and a little rough round the edges. Even tired out cynical atheists will cheer when the lights of the Cathedral pop back on at the end after the old pagan wizard fixes the fuses...

NB. The right thing to do with this serial is to begin it six weeks before Christmas Eve, eking it out gradually. This will mean your Christmas TV viewing will begin mid-November. This is no bad thing.

Ha, ha, what?

Cagney and Lacey

Episode Title: I'll be Home for Christmas

Channel: BBC 1

Original UK Transmission Date: 17 June 1983

Regular Cast: Tyne Daly (Mary Beth Lacey), Sharon Gless (Christine Cagney), Al Waxman (Lt. Bert Samuels), Carl Lumby (Mark Petrie), Martin Kove (Victor Isbecki), Sindey Clute (Paul La Guardia), John Karlen (Harvey Lacey), Troy Slaten (Michael Lacey), Tony La Torre (Harvey Lacey Jr)

Guest Cast: John Del Regno (Myer Rudolpho), Ned Glass (Pickpocket), Lyla Graham (Doris Rainey), Michael C Gwynne (Phillip Malik), Richard Masur (Ralph Barbinski), Barry Primus (Sgt. Dory McKenna), Milton Selzer (Willie Boxer), Suzanne Stone (Claudia Petrie)

Writer: Robert Crais

Director: Burt Brinckerhoff

Christmas Eve at the 14th Precinct finds everyone eager to get home for the holidays until an escaped criminal dressed as Santa complicates matters.

Only now, after many repeated viewings of *I'll Be Home for Christmas* from **Cagney and Lacey**'s first season, do I realise that it's a partial rewrite – or at least an homage to – *The Blue*

Carbuncle from the Sherlock Holmes stories. Not in terms of what goes on, perhaps, but in its atmosphere and ethos: the fact that it's a detective story happening in the very last hours of Christmas Eve, and it finishes with the crooks being forgiven and sent home, unpunished – their crimes seeming petty and forgivable in the festive circumstances.

In a sense, every good detective story is already a homage to Holmes, of course, and **Cagney and Lacey** echoes the shape of those tales, in that each episode consists of a series of forays out from their base in the precinct into the busy city around them. Just like Holmes and Watson our ladies visit the highest and the lowest in all kinds of locales. Here, they're visiting not the pubs of Bloomsbury or the market stalls of the East End, but the tenements of the Lower East Side and the glitzy shopping emporiums of midtown Manhattan.

It's an episode about a Santa Claus impersonator – a family man with learning difficulties – who gets locked up for cracking parking meters and bagging the cash. Somehow he manages to escape from the cells in the precinct and the Captain is forced to cancel everyone's annual leave until he is found. The episode is about his escape and his capture and, I suppose, if we were to draw the parallel again with the Holmes story, our Santa is the equivalent of the stolen dead goose.

Cagney and Lacey was not only a great show for boasting two strong female leads, it was also a great ensemble piece and in this episode each of the regulars gets a moment to shine. Mary Beth and Christine are always utterly believable – Cagney slightly racy with her sexy boyfriends and her alcohol problems. Lacey was the devoted Italian mama full of absolute good sense, and never afraid to tear a strip off anyone. As the hours tick down on Christmas Eve this episode is really about how their fierce devotion to policing can take over their entire lives, as Cagney's boyfriend is left drinking wine and decorating the tree alone (longing to taste her plum pudding, he tells her on the phone...!) and Mary Beth's boys celebrate Christmas Eve with their father, the placidly ursine Harvey. There's a brief visit home, in the middle of it all, and a touching present-giving, but all of this is secondary to the job in hand. They keep praying for nothing further to go wrong, for no more felonies to be carried out in their presence, forcing them back into the precinct, but this is New York and the place is awash with all kinds of dubious activity. It seems like they'll never get home.

It's the small character moments that shine – Petrie waiting to hear about his wife giving birth, and the dramas over her complications. Old La Guardia having to miss a performance of Handel's **Messiah**, and his lady friend waiting patiently at the station for him. She gets flirted at by Lieutenant Samuels, who drags her off to his office and plies her with the gallon-sized bottle of eggnog he's been lugging around all day. His fit of pique when his helicopter toy breaks (his staff have presented it to him in order to pacify him) is priceless.

The guest star is the errant Santa Claus played by Richard Masur (coincidentally, also a guest player in **The Story Lady**, as we'll see later on) and he makes a lovely job of bringing a kind of selfish innocence to the role. He sees nothing wrong in taking the cash he needs from parking meters, in order to travel to Florida for an opportunity in Crazy Golf. We see the in-laws his small family must cohabit with, and our heart goes out to him because his wife's father clearly hates his guts. Cagney and Lacey share our feelings.

Snow falls thickly, even when it isn't supposed to. Santa steals a patrol car and tries to launder cash with an elf selling fir trees. There's even childbirth in the closing moments, just before the credits roll. Was there ever a show that made you feel as much like you were in New York City at Christmas as this one?

Camp Christmas

Episode Title: Camp Christmas

Channel: Channel 4

Original UK Transmission Date: 24 December 1993

Regular Cast: Andy Bell (Host), Melissa Etheridge (Host)

Guest Cast: Pedro Almodovar (Himself), Sandra Bernhard (Herself), Simon Callow (Himself), Julian Clary (Talking Reindeer), Quentin Crisp (Himself), Lea DeLaria (Herself), Justin Fashanu (Himself), Stephen Fry (Himself), Derek Jarman (Himself), Armistead Maupin (Himself), Sir Ian McKellen (Himself), Martina Navratilova (Herself), Paul O'Grady (Lily Savage), Mark Trevorrow (Bob Downe)

Channel 4's alternative Christmas celebration hosted by Erasure's Andy Bell and American singer Melissa Etheridge, starring Stephen Fry, Quentin Crisp, Martina Navratilova, Ian McKellen, Pam St Clement, Polly Perkins and Julian Clary as a talking reindeer.

I remember this so clearly. Channel 4, late at night, Christmas 1993. It was a big deal, because there was going to be an actual gay-themed Christmas special, with actual gay and lesbian stars of stage and screen and everything.

26

This is like looking back down the wrong end of a telescope, watching **Camp Christmas** today. In some ways, it should be funny because we should be able to say 'we've come so far since then.' And it's true, that some of the jokes and tropes used in **Camp Christmas** could be found almost anywhere in mainstream culture today, and the whole production is far less risqué than it seemed back in the early Nineties. At the same time, however, it sharpens my sense of things we have lost, and makes me wonder if we aren't, in some ways, moving backwards.

The special is set within a cosy log cabin in snowy woods. It's a set-up from an Andy Williams or Val Doonican Christmas special. The idea is to pretend our hosts are inviting their guests to stay with them for the holidays. There'll be songs and fun and sentimental silliness. Andy Bell and Melissa Etheridge throw themselves into the role of hosts, with only Erasure's Andy looking dubious now and then. When they sing Julie Andrews together in front of the log fire he looks a bit like a robot teddy bear. He wants a bigger space in which to gyrate than this living room. Melissa seems quite at home, whipping out her guitar to give everyone 'Santa Claus is Coming to Town.' She seems comfy at a homely shindig.

It's the Nineties, so irony is at an eye-wateringly high level. The moments that work best are when people arrive in character and whoop it up hilariously. Bob Downe gets the tone right, towards the end, gracing the living room with his presence and belting out his song as if he was on stage in Vegas, while trampling on the coffee table and draping himself on people's laps. Paul O' Grady as Lily Savage is note perfect, too, arriving with the buffet and snapping out some wonderful one-liners that would work in any era. 'Hang onto the clingfilm in case there's an orgy later.'

It's the people who are there as themselves who seem a bit awkward. They are left hanging round, making this special seem a bit off. Justin Fashanu, the out footballing hero of the age. is called upon to do his party piece, which is a duff card trick, and this falls flat. There's a female colonel who's been chucked out of the US military, who turns up to have her story told – rightfully so – but she's no performer and looks like she's been stunned with a brick. It all sits uneasily beside Stephen Fry arriving as Santa, doing his own ribald party piece and not really connecting with anyone at all.

There's the frail and nodding figure of legendary, dying film director, Derek Jarman, on screen throughout this show. He sits with a blanket over his lap, a little hat on his head. A benign spectre at the feast. Most new arrivals say hello, but he's a conspicuously quiet figure, struggling to stay in the moment. He's doggedly hanging in there, taking part in what must have seemed like a big stride forward for gay people on TV.

Again, Lily Savage judges the moment just right. While others are talking she takes a plate of sandwiches round, which he shakes his head at. 'I'll get you some cake later,' she tells him. It's a moment of piercing, lovely truth in the middle of all the awkward artifice.

At the end of the show they gather to sing 'Have Yourself a Merry Little Christmas', from **Meet Me in St Louis**. Those words – because they were sung by Judy Garland in the first place – have always had a wonderfully bittersweet resonance for gay people. The idea of someday soon 'we all will be together' seems to chime off the idea that this is a winter cottage for all people to feel safe in: that there is an actual place where we will eventually be together, even if it's a heavily ironic, parodic, borrowed place. This is coupled in these verses with that lovely line about 'until then we'll have to muddle through somehow' – a line I've always found indescribably moving. Again, it describes the lives of gay and lesbian people the world over with wonderful clarity.

We do muddle through somehow. Subversively, covertly sometimes, other times out in the open and through glorious art, music, cultural revolutions. We muddle and we struggle and it's a story that's developing and changing all the time. In 'gay years' this TV show is already a hundred years away. So much has changed. So much has moved forward. But so much has slipped backwards. We've lost so many people and so many ideals since then.

Camp Christmas is a piece of whimsical nonsense. But like many festive shows it's a time capsule. A little bubble of golden light in the winter dark. It might look cheesy and rubbish when you peer through the windows, but it was the Nineties. We elevated naffness to an art form. We worshipped irony and silliness for its own sake. It was a fin-de-siècle thing. Everything has become so much more earnest and professionalised and slick since then, it seems. The tinselly amateurism of a show like this seems more daring now than any of its proud gayness.

Christmas Spirits

Episode Title: Christmas Spirits

Channel: ITV

Original UK Transmission Date: 1 January 1981

Cast: Elaine Stritch (Julia Myerson), Ben Aris (Charles Aintry), Stephanie Cole (Mrs Purvis), Norma West (Angela Aintrey)

Writer: Willis Hall

Director: June Wyndham-Davies

Julia, a Hollywood property scout, is looking for a house to star in a horror movie, she finds more than she bargained for at Glebes Hall.

Someone at ITV must have looked across at the BBC and thought, 'Well, we can do that. All those marvelous **Ghost Stories for Christmas**. So chilly and creepy and full of class. Why, we should have our own ITV version. We just need a mansion and some wintry twilight. Throw in some half-hidden, frightful things. We'll conjure up an hour of unbearable tension and crank it up to a ghastly climax. Now, who shall we get to star? Denholm Elliot? Michael Hordern?

No. Let's ask Elaine Stritch.

Will she look ashen and bleakly haunted? Will she bring some gravitas to this eerie tale?

Or will she shamble about the place like a crazy lady in clumpy shoes and a beige tunic dress doing jazz hands and squawking at the top of her voice?'

This has to be one of my favourite hours of TV ever. Stritch plays a location researcher for a US film company, coming to stay in the wilds of the English countryside, in order to check out a spooky mansion for a horror film. She is welcomed by a couple who are trying to make a buck out of their dilapidated stately pile. They're keen to tell the world about the ghostly, murderous children haunting their hall.

Elaine's character, Julia, is entranced by the whole place. This is real England. She sits on their sofa, knocking back whisky, smoking fags, cackling and congratulating herself on her good fortune.

The only trouble is that the resident spirits and the Mrs Danvers-like housekeeper (a completely terrifying Stephanie Cole) aren't best pleased.

Julia's hosts are a bickering couple. The willowy, aristocratic lady has married beneath herself, and he's a conniving, oiky presence, wonderfully snarky as he curries favour with their visitor. He's desperate for the cash her film folk will bring and he's bitterly resentful of his predicament, living off crumbs in the corner of this drafty estate. He takes great relish in playing up the ghostly horrors of the place, describing them until their guest has to tamp down her fear with more fags and booze.

Is it tasteless to suggest I care more for Willis Hall's characters than I do for any of M R James'? There's just something so true about this horrible lot.

Then, of course, Julia finds herself alone on Christmas Eve. Her hosts nip out on a visit, their car breaks down, and Julia has to spend an evening alone in the haunted mansion. At first she's pragmatic and full of bravado. Her interior monologue rings out loudly through the dusky studio set. Then she manages to lock herself out of the cosy living quarters. Then the lights and heating go off. Then she starts hearing the ghostly giggles from the upper rooms and soon we are racketing about with her in a full-blown nightmare.

Poor old Elaine Stritch dashes up and down the wooden staircases, rather quickly going out of her mind. She flaps and shrieks like a banshee. The whole thing is a ghoulishly silly delight.

There are at least two massive, jumpy scares. Much bigger than anything we get in the BBC M.R. James plays. Seriously. You can forget your dripping ichor and your wraithlike figures on the beach. There are two moments here that are so frightening that Elaine Stritch is struck almost dumb.

Christmas Spirits has more than its fair share of those delicious moments that make you want to laugh as much as you cry out in fear.

The whole thing is meant to be terribly serious, of course. It's never played for laughs. But there's something irresistibly hilarious about Stritch – this frazzled old broad – smoking and boozing her way through a nasty Christmas visitation.

Coronation Street

Episode Title: Episode 1872

Channel: ITV

Original UK Transmission Date: 27 December 1978

Regular Cast: Jack Howarth (Albert Tatlock), William Roache (Ken Barlow), Geoffrey Hughes (Eddie Yeats), Jean Alexander (Hilda Ogden), Bernard Youens (Stan Ogden), Anne Kirkbride (Deirdre Langton), Peter Adamson (Len Fairclough), Violet Carson (Ena Sharples), Christabel Finch (Tracy Langton), Patricia Phoenix (Elsie Tanner), Helen Worth (Gail Potter), Julie Goodyear (Bet Lynch), Doris Speed (Annie Walker), Betty Driver (Betty Turpin), Eileen Derbyshire (Emily Bishop), Christopher Quinten (Brian Tilsley)

Guest Cast: Joe Lynch (Ron Mather), Catherine Neilson (Karen Barnes), Ray Ashcroft (Tim Gibbs), Russell Dickson (Dave Barnes), William Tarmey (Jack Rowe)

Writer: John Stevenson

Director: Jeremy Summers

My favourite episodes of **Coronation Street** were the party ones, in which someone would say, 'Let's all go back to mine!' and the rest of the episode would take place in a sitting room much too small for the assembled guests.

Seventies **Corrie** looks slightly bleak now, with its shabby furniture and brown walls and dowdy polyester clothes. Suddenly we are reminded that the Seventies are so much closer to World War Two than they are to today and we see that for the likes of Elsie Tanner – whose party this is – that wartime era was their heyday. This flame-haired temptress had a wonderful war, if we are to believe the gossip and whispered backstory on the Street.

Elsie has had this party sprung on her by her Irish boyfriend, who got carried away down the pub, inviting all and sundry to an impromptu shindig. When she hears about it, she doesn't mind at all. She's happy for the whole street to descend on her house, bringing a bottle and having a little dance. First they have to pull all the furniture back against the wall and clear the sideboard to put all the drink on.

Things seem so simple back then. People were happy with so little. Look at barmaid Bet Lynch in her shiny black pencil skirt. She's gyrating away like she's dancing 'Saturday Night Fever' with John Travolta, and in her head, that's exactly what she's doing. Prim and proper Emily Bishop daringly asks for a glass of home-brewed rhubarb wine instead of her usual 'small sherry' and she likes it so much she ends up downing the rest of the bottle and sits slightly squiffily on Elsie's uncomfortable settee, enjoying the party as it unfolds around her. Poor Emily was never in the swing of things more than this evening in 1978.

Even gate-crashers, even complete strangers wandering into your home, aren't anything to be worried about. Two young fellas slope in, hoping to pick up women. Elsie welcomes them warmly, thinking that they don't look like such bad lads. One of them turns out to be Brian Tilsley, who here meets Gail Potter for the first time. Gail is the lodger of Elsie, who will turn out to be the matriarch of a troubled dynasty whose ups and downs will keep us glued to the screen for the next four decades. It's a massive moment in **Corrie** history, this meeting of Gail and Brian. (He's an awful actor, right from the first. He's actually **too** much like someone who's just walked in off the street...)

In today's show there would have to be sudden death and disaster at a do like this. A plane would come hurtling out of the skies to crash on Weatherfield, trapping the locals for days under the rubble of their homes. Or the young man who walks Deidre home would turn out to be an armed gunman, a crazy terrorist. A series of unspeakable things would lead to nightly instalments through a whole week, perhaps, and we would be kept guessing who will manage to survive **Corrie**'s bleakest and most bloody Christmas yet.

But, no. It's 1978. This is a gentle affair set to a disco soundtrack. Cheesy music and home brew and the only note of discord being the shrill grumbles from Hilda next door, piqued because she wasn't invited. Jean Alexander steals the show, as usual, with her single scene: a disgruntled harpie hunched in front of her telly, feeling left out, as always.

I always loved **Corrie** best when they kept it very simple. The best bits are when they put the whole cast in a small room and let them behave and interact, and allow us to eavesdrop on the fun. In some ways, that's what I like best about **all** TV.

Crossroads

Episode Title: Episode 3235

Channel: ITV

Original UK Transmission Date: 31 December 1979

Regular Cast: Noele Gordon (Meg Mortimer), Alan Gifford (Lloyd Munro), Jane Rossington (Jill Harvey), Sorrel Dunger (Sarah Jane Harvey), Susan Hanson (Diane Hunter), Bruce Lidington (P.C. Steve Cater), Magda Miller (Patricia Blake), Stephen Thorne (Ch. Supt. Blake), Ivor Salter (Reg Cotterill), Carina Wyeth (Alison Cotterill), Tony Brooks (Leonard Hobson), Kathy Staff (Doris Luke), Ronald Allen (David Hunter), Janet Hargreave (Rosemary Hunter), Roger Tonge (Sandy Richardson), Joy Andrews (Tish Hope), Sue Lloyd (Barbara Brady), Lynette McMorrough (Glenda Brownlow), Elisabeth Croft (Miss Tatum)

Writers: Michala Crees, David Garfield and Arthur Schmidt

Director: Geoff Husson

Alison and Leonard attend the hospital party, much to Reg's disdain. Meg throws a select Christmas Day soiree for her family and friends.

When I was a kid the Crossroads Motel at 6pm every weekday was the safest place in the world, at least until 1981, when they burned it down.

It didn't matter where you were – at home, a grandparent's house, with aunties or at a friend's – that same theme would come on and be instantly reassuring. Those particular rooms – the foyer with its mural of the queen and fake floral arrangement, the motel kitchens, Meg's olive green sitting room (which was the height of sophistication) – it was all very lovely and familiar. These were the sites of trauma, betrayal, death and disaster, obviously, but they were still some of the happier places TV could take you to.

At Christmas this cosy factor increased a hundredfold. In those days it didn't seem like Christmas until you had caught up with what was happening in King's Oak and the Motel. There were certain **Crossroads** rituals each year, such as mention of the village carol service and seeing presents exchanged between regulars and glasses of sherry raised in toast. Paramount, though, was seeing Noele Gordon – Motel boss Meg Mortimer – in her white fur coat and hat. It was glamorous and vast (could it possibly have once belonged to a polar bear?) and she donned it once a year not so much to show off, but to be glam for the sake of her people: the humble denizens of the Midlands town where she ruled the roost so benignly.

There is a story that the fur coat was actually the property of the actress, Noele Gordon herself, and it was she, just as much as Meg, who liked to be seen wearing it in each year's Christmas show. She wanted us all to see how well she had done in her twenty-odd years of TV stardom. We were all the humble folk of King's Oak to her and, grateful subjects that we were, we voted Nolly TV Personality of the Year annually through the Seventies in the *TV Times* poll[1].

Nolly was magnificent, of course, in the way she held all the ramshackle parts of this show together. It didn't matter how hokey or bogus all the other strands of story were, so long as you had a scene or two with Meg in her big glasses and a two piece suit or cardigan and skirt ensemble, with her shock of red hair hard as a meringue, then all was right with the world. The programme had a heart.

Only a year or two after this Christmas 1979 episode they would write her out – against her will – in a move that was shocking

---

[1] Noele Gordon won the *TV Times* 'Most Popular Television Actress' award eight times in the Seventies.
[2] The entire cast – with the exception of Stephen Thorne as Aslan – was different for the US version of the cartoon.
[3] First shown in the United States on 16 December 1987.

and daring and ultimately disastrous. They burned down the old motel and revamped everything for the Eighties and though it went on for a further seven years, it was never the same again without its charismatic matriarch. The ghost of that polar bear coat visited each Christmas and found the Eighties lacking.

When I first became aware of **Crossroads** online fandom there was a heartbreaking series of photos someone had taken of the window display of a charity shop in a suburb of Birmingham. Here was an identical fur coat and hat, sleek and glossy and ivory white. Still as wonderful as they ever were on TV, or in the pages of the *TV Times*. But in twenty-first century Britain they had no home and no owner. The charity shop seemed to know what they had on their hands; indeed, there was a label inside the coat, giving the name of the fancy furrier and Ms Gordon herself. It was genuine and authenticated.

The fans came to the shop to pay homage. They took photos. They asked to touch the coat. They even tried it on, and took more pictures. They talked among themselves online. Someone should stump up the cash. They should have a whip round. They could hold a raffle. Maybe there was lottery funding for something like this? It was a piece of our nation's heritage, wasn't it? The discussion went on for some days, in the internet forums. Then, by the time the original poster returned to the shop to have a talk with the charity people about what might be done, of course the hat and coat were gone. The window was displaying some other ensemble: something of no historical interest whatsoever.

Like the Snow Queen in the old, festive tale, she had vanished overnight. Maybe it was better that way? Nolly only ever appeared in this guise once a year. If she was trapped forever in a museum, say, we couldn't imagine that she was leading a glamorous life aboard the QE2 or in Venice. That's how I like to picture Meg or Nolly now. (Perhaps she's abroad with her real life best chum, Larry Grayson. Perhaps they're both wearing fur coats and hats and flitting around the world?)

The story of the coat came to light about the time that Network DVD (blessed be their name) released the first **Crossroads** boxed sets and it was rather like going to visit a branch of the family you hadn't seen for twenty five years, and perhaps thought you never would. Some family members you'd even – to your embarrassment – forgotten altogether. (This is the nature of archive TV. It's all about reunions that can be both mortifying as well as joyful. 'Oh, I remember you! You were in that dreadful show we all adored! Yes, wasn't it wonderful? It's still happening! It's all still happening forever!')

So I rediscovered the Christmas episode for 1979 and, though I can't claim to have remembered all its specifics, the feeling was familiar. It's at the very end of the seventies and the cast is converging on Meg's sitting room for an afternoon party and a glass of sherry. With hindsight it feels terrible that no one knows that this is one of the last times they will all be together. Soon enough the motel will be in cinders and everyone will think Meg has perished in the flames (though she doesn't, she escapes onto a cruise liner bound for warmer climes.) Also, David Hunter, the slightly creaky catalogue model-handsome motel manager will leave his icily-polite wife Rosemary and within the year she will go completely bananas. She will confront him on the night of his engagement to his new wife and shoot him through the heart. He will drop lifeless onto the rug in his office and bleed bright pink blood. Then we'll get some very exciting episodes with everyone guessing who-shot-David-Hunter which are, presumably, all the idea of an incoming producer who wants very much to spice things up.

And so, with the change in decade, we get infernos and attempted murders. If the 1979 cast knew what was just around the corner – if they knew their numbers would be so cruelly culled – they'd be drinking something stronger than sherry at Meg's little shindig.

But there is no hint of ominous foreshadowing here. This is still the seventies and we can revel in the glorious mundanity of it all. Meg's daughter Jill and her docile toddler Sarah Jane (utterly unaware that she'll turn out to be bitter and evil in the 2001 revival of the show) open presents and chambermaid Miss Diane brings a humble gift of her own. **Crossroads** always seemed a bit feudal, with Meg and her family acting as a benign aristocracy, their staff very loyal to the Richardson family. Here, Miss Diane is cockahoop because Jill has bought her a bottle of scent. Later, Miss Luke stares at Meg with an expression of such overwhelming Sapphic devotion that you feel like you're intruding on a private moment (though it could simply be that the camera is slow to pan round the room during the party and poor Kathy Staff is caught in a rictus of reaction).

It's lovely watching an episode of a soap out of context. You get the loose ends of plots you'll never see resolved, and glimpse secondary and tertiary characters whose stories you'll never understand. Just what is going on between the agitated woman in the bar, arguing with her perplexed husband? She wants a divorce but she's cryptic (and possibly not in full possession of her lines). The husband is played by Stephen Thorne, who once played both Omega and Azal the Dæmon in early seventies **Doctor Who**, and it's very odd to hear him having something as banal as a marital altercation in a motel reception. Which spouse would dare to risk the wrath of a cosmic super god?

Then there's the whole sub plot about the girl with the oddly-dyed hair and speech impediment, and how her bullish, puritanical father grudgingly allows her to escape from their cottage for a couple of hours on Christmas Day. She is taken to a party at the local hospital by her awkward gentleman friend, a male nurse called Leonard, who whisks her away. The old farmer glowers at the very idea of his daughter having fun. Even though everything about these scenes is hamfisted and shonky, there is something wonderful about them. I want to know whether this girl ever escaped from her blighted life – perhaps with the help of Leonard in his beige slacks, or Doris Luke, who is a close family friend. Does her gruff father ever stop treating her like a slave? Her story exists in a little bubble of bittersweet and temporary joy. It's a fairy tale glittering in the soapy lather.

And so we come to the end of the episode and one of the most joyous and absurd moments I've ever witnessed on British TV. It should be awful and cheesy and lame and in some ways that's exactly what Meg's Christmas soiree is. The whole cast is assembled on the too-small set of her living room. There are classic Seventies tinsel decorations. Meg has shed her fur coat and is fussing round, seeing that the assembled horde is

46

supplied with drink and platefuls of mini sausage rolls and crisps. Toddler Sarah Jane stares abstractly into the distance as the adults chatter – she's clearly planning her future evil deeds.

Motel staff mingle freely with old friends and local tycoons. Meg is grinning warmly at them all – beatifically – and she's at the centre of the world she has created.

Someone rashly asks her to give them all a song.

'Oh, I couldn't,' she demurs – briefly.

'Go on!' the cast of **Crossroads** insists.

Possibly they have noticed the four-piece jazz troupe who have set up their instruments in the corner of Meg's salon.

'Key of D, John,' she commands.

Then she starts to sing.

And the band plays along.

What is it? A hymn? A carol?

She hits the chorus. She swings round to face the room and the camera zooms in for a huge close-up of her grinning face as she sings 'We Need a Little Christmas' from the hit musical, **Mame**.

She sings it like she's onstage at the London Palladium. If the room wasn't so small everyone would take a couple of steps backwards. Those sitting down look like they're being blasted by a force nine gale. Sausage roll crumbs fly from their party plates. Tinsel garlands shiver at the roar of her voice.

It's glorious. It blasts down the fourth wall. It turns the humdrum little drama – just for a moment – into a glittering Variety show. It ends the episode, the year and the decade in wonderful, slightly tacky style.

It's still a shock, each time I watch this episode, every Christmas Eve. Is she really going to pull it off? Is she going to be persuaded to sing to them yet again?

I love the thought that there's always a fragment of Christmas 1979 that never ends, in which everyone still has a glass of sherry and a handful of salted nuts. A Christmas Eve on which we're still watching this woman with a very loud voice and orange lipstick, braying out a Broadway number in her sitting room. And meanwhile everyone else sits or stands in awe of her, feeling themselves forced to sing along.

Good old Meg. Good old **Crossroads**.

Doctor Who

Episode Title: The Christmas Invasion

Channel: BBC 1

Original UK Transmission Date: 25 December 2005

Regular Cast: David Tennant (The Doctor), Billie Piper (Rose Tyler)

Guest Cast: Camille Coduri (Jackie Tyler), Noel Clarke (Mickey Smith), Penelope Wilton (Harriet Jones), Adam Garcia (Alex), Daniel Evans (Danny Llewellyn), Sean Gilder (Sycorax Leader), Anita Briem (Sally Jacobs), Chu Omambala (Major Blake), Sian McDowell (Sandra), Paul Anderson (Jason), Cathy Murphy (Mum), Sean Carlsen (Policeman), Jason Mohammad (Newsreader 1), Sagar Arya (Newsreader 2), Lachele Carl (Newsreader 3)

Writer: Russell T Davies

Director: James Hawes

It is Christmas, but there is little cause for celebration as planet Earth is invaded by aliens known as the Sycorax. It is up to Rose and the newly regenerated Doctor to save humanity, with a bit of help from her boyfriend Mickey and her mother Jackie.

There's a lot to be said about *The Christmas Invasion* and, like almost every **Doctor Who** episode ever made, a lot of it has already been said. (Really, has there ever been a TV show so exhaustively documented and analysed?) I think the most important thing to say about it here is that it's the story when **Doctor Who** at last came home. In 1981 or 1974 or 1975 or 1967 it would have been hard to imagine the Doctor sitting down to Christmas lunch with an ordinary family in a council flat at the end of his adventure, but here it feels wonderfully right.

In 2005 **Doctor Who** was still newly back on TV. It was a big hit and it was suddenly the jewel in the BBC's crown and at the heart of their Christmas Day schedule. But it was still relatively new to vast swathes of the audience. Christmas Day is, of course, when more people watch TV than any other day and so this episode would be seen by people who perhaps hadn't yet caught up with this revived, updated iteration of the show.

When I was a kid – in the late Tom Baker years and the Peter Davison era – I longed for a **Doctor Who** special on Christmas Day. Looking back at the schedules, Christmas telly could be pretty ropey back then – lots of dodgy old movies, feature-length specials of sitcoms that had very little to do with Christmas at all, and Noel Edmonds broadcasting live from the top of the Telecom tower. It would have been mind-boggling to the twelve year old me, the very idea of a long **Who** episode about London being invaded by Christmas-themed voodoo aliens. I couldn't have imagined whole families sitting down to watch it together. I was still at the stage where watching **Doctor Who** was an almost clinical operation – you absorbed all the details in silence; you listened repeatedly to your home-recorded soundtrack afterwards, thinking it all over in great depth, hoping to make sense of the story, and praying for it to be good.

2005 is still a strange thing, looking back. The idea of nearly everyone watching **Doctor Who** feels just weird. As weird as waking up and the whole world being hypnotized by aliens and milling about in their pyjamas. What's more, everyone was watching what is, essentially, a UNIT adventure that might have occurred back in the days of Jon Pertwee. Except this time a lot of the tale was played out against the backdrop of a council estate and this is the thing that would have been most mind-blowing of all to the twelve year old me, who had spent his whole life living on council estates. **Doctor Who** had come home – to my home in particular, it seemed like.

Jackie Tyler and Rose and Mickey and Harriet Jones – those are the characters that make this episode sing with wonderful, believable life. As well, of course, as David Tennant debuting his Doctor in his jim-jams, weaving about the place like a hyperactive otter. The story crackles along and plays very much

52

to its audience – knowing that it will find them sated with Christmas dinner, slightly drunk, fizzing with sugar rush; possibly over-stimulated and teary. And what this audience wants to see are killer Father Christmas robots and evil Christmas trees that whir and scythe into deadly life.

In the years since then **Doctor Who** has become an inevitable feature of Christmas Day telly and only occasionally has it hit the same heights again. Wonderful guest stars such as Kylie Minogue, John Simm or Michael Gambon have elevated some of these specials, but sometimes they've proved to be just a bit too throwaway and lightweight, and sometimes they forget they're playing to the general audience that lapped up *The Christmas Invasion* so keenly.

I love the fact that we can be nostalgic already about 2005. The way the twenty-first century is rushing by, it already seems like 1975. The Britain that the Sycorax wanted to invade already seems rather quaint and that's fitting, I suppose, for an episode that slots within the genre of 'cosy catastrophe.' There's nothing too harrowing here. Just a near-collision with Christmas Day disaster, and a new Doctor saving the world, all over again.

Emu's World

Episode Title: Emu's World at Christmas

Channel: BBC 1

Original UK Transmission Date: 21 December 1983

Regular Cast: Rod Hull (Himself / King Boggle / Emu)

Guest Cast: Carol Lee Scott (Grotbags), Freddie Stevens (Croc / Sergeant), Susan Maughan (Princess Hortensia), Carl Wayne (Odd Job John)

Writer: Rod Hull

Director: Colin Clews

Grotbags lures Rod and Emu into a trap involving a magical roundabout. She wants to give the bird to the Magnificent Fred at his Grand Christmas Ball. But her Hovergrot goes down near Boggle's Kingdom.

The very week that I'm writing this chapter, news comes through about the woman who played Grotbags – Carol Lee Scott – dying in her mid seventies. Grotbags was a fabulous, bright-green battleaxe. She galumphed about the screen, singing fabulously and cackling like a crazy lady. She was the perfect foil for Rod Hull and his mutely savage Emu puppet.

Rod Hull was kind of a zany Willy Wonka figure. He clearly cast himself in the Pied Piper mould, tramping about, leading hordes of stage brat kids about the countryside in dance numbers and dashing about inside the Pink Windmill. When we think of him now, though, we can't separate him from his ultimate demise, just before the turn of the century, clambering onto the roof of his house to adjust his TV aerial in a storm. Then dropping to his death into the garden below. Is it wrong of me to imagine – as I have done ever since 1999 – that a certain puppet, banished to the attic as he apparently was, managed to snake his head out of a skylight window and goose his long-term master as he struggled with his reception? Is that quite the wrong thing to picture?

When Grotbags karked it Facebook was filled with pictures of her lurid mush and bubble perm. People were remembering Emu's shows with great fondness. It struck me that she was one of the unsung heroes of telly. When we look back she might not be one of the first faces and voices we think of, but she's certainly there, in our own individual archives. I wonder if she even knew how fondly now-middle aged people remember her turn as that witch, with her camp crocodile and robot sidekicks and her flying hoover? It was a pantomime turn that she reprised in the Nineties, in a show of her own, but the episodes I'm thinking about here are the Christmas specials of the early

Eighties, in which Emu was her nemesis and she had some lovely songs and some sparky lines. She might be gone from the real world now, but in these old Christmassy shows, she's alive forever.

Fame

Episode Title: All I Want for Christmas

Channel: BBC 1

Original UK Transmission Date: 8 December 1986

Regular Cast: Debbie Allen (Lydia Grant), Carlo Imperato (Danny Amatullo), Gene Anthony Ray (Leroy Johnson), Albert Hague (Mr. Benjamin Shorofsky), Ann Nelson (Mrs. Berg), Carol Mayo Jenkins (Elizabeth Sherwood), Bill Hufsey (Christopher Donlon), Valerie Landsburg (Doris Schwartz),

Guest Cast: Caryn Ward (Tina), Zachary Bostrom (Timmy), Elden Ratliff (Matthew), Dick Miller (Lou Mackie), Tony DiBenedetto (Mr. Quimby), John Ingle (Man In Hospital Suite 2B), Carolyn J. Silas (Laura Mackie), Myrna White (Nurse), Carl Bressler (Pickpocket), Garette Ratliff (Youngster)

Writer: Robert Caplain

Director: Alan Myerson

Tina pays Leroy, who is busy studying, a surprise visit for Christmas when her dad goes out of town. Leroy intends to buy her the $300 doll house that she wants but is robbed and so is forced to take a second job. Unfortunately, Leroy ends up spending no time with Tina, in spite of his good intentions.

Professor Shorofsky is hospitalised for Christmas when he has to have his tonsils out. Two children in the hospital, Timmy and Matthew, think he's Santa Claus, much to his initial disgust, but in the end he comes around.

By 1986 the Kids from Fame were mostly grown-up and gone. They were either famous or they'd disco-danced their way back into obscurity. Their heyday had been around 1983 when they sang 'Hi-Fidelity' and 'Starmaker' and released albums, did live shows, and there were even annuals featuring further adventures of the irrepressible, leg-warmer-wearing youngsters.

I absolutely loved this series in its early days because it was nothing like our school. In the early Eighties in the north-east, industrial action by all our teachers meant that there were no after-school activities at all. Before we'd all arrived at Woodham Comp they'd had Christmas shows in which everyone took part – 'Dracula Spectacular' was the one everyone talked about. But by the time we were there: zilch. There was no singing and dancing on stage, in the corridors or anywhere. Even after the teachers' strikes were over, there were still no after-school activities. Just homework and the occasional fight on the school fields.

Fame opened up a whole world of doing stuff in school; the novel idea of actually doing stuff that you really loved. (There were things we did at school that I really loved, but even I knew that there was nothing intrinsically spectacular, or worthy of televising or devising a programme around 'Reading!' or 'Painting with Water Colours!')

The other thing about **Fame** was to do with the allure of its setting. It paints a wonderful picture of New York City. It's vibrant and diverse and no one minds if hordes of kids do song and dance numbers all over the place. It's not the scary place that the cop shows of the time would have had you believe.

By 1986 and the Christmas episode, *All I Want for Christmas*, there's a new crop of students who are, regrettably, much less interesting than the original cast. This doesn't stop this episode from being a wonderful sentimental piece of enjoyable nonsense.

It's snowy in NYC – which is the best place outside of Lapland to see snow in – and there's a street set in this episode that Leroy dances all over during the show-stopping number. He also sings the number, which is ghastly and a mistake. At this point in the series Leroy has become a teacher at the school. He's studying to pass exams, working too hard and going a bit grumpy with stress. His sassy kid cousin Tina arrives for a visit (or has she runaway from an unhappy home?) and we learn that she's been deprived of happy Christmases all her life. He wants to ensure she has a great time this year. Soon he learns that what she'd really like is the three hundred dollar dolls' house they see in a toyshop window. Leroy throws everything into raising the required amount of cash. But he ends up working so hard it all goes a bit counterproductive and he snaps nastily at the kid. He leaves her to decorate the Christmas tree alone. In his singlemindedness he has forgotten what Christmas is really all about. Whoops.

Professor Shorofsky, meanwhile, is in hospital having his tonsils removed. He's in a ward full of precocious children who become convinced the old man is really Santa. He barks and glowers at them, but by the end his heart has melted and he dresses up and throws a party on the ward. Every character from this episode attends, and Leroy's niece gets to help Santa dispensing presents and so has a nice time anyway. It's all idiotically heart-warming and sweet, of course, but there's just something nice about **Fame**. And I'm glad that the old lady secretary, Mrs Berg, is still there in 1986.

Frasier

Episode Title: Perspectives on Christmas

Channel: Channel 4

Original UK Transmission Date: 6 March 1998

Regular Cast: Kelsey Grammer (Frasier Crane), David Hyde-Pierce (Niles Crane), Jane Leeves (Daphne Moon), John Mahoney (Martin Crane)

Guest Cast: Albert Macklin (Masseur), Conrad Janis Albert), Brooks Almy (Mother in Elevator), Marilyn O'Connor (Albert's Wife), Jennifer Williams (Woman in Hall), Mark Capri (Man in Hall), Jamie Alexis (Sally), J.B. Gaynor (Billy), Zachary McLemore (Big Kid)

Writer: Christopher Lloyd

Director: David Lee

During a massage session designed to combat holiday stress, each member of the extended Crane family relates the story of the last few days, with their individual perspectives creating subtle differences.

Frasier's Christmas episode was an annual tradition in each of the show's eleven seasons between 1993 and 2004. There is something extra special about these instalments, with each of the leads reverting to type – perhaps a little more exaggeratedly than usual. There's a slightly manic edge, perhaps, to do with these characters' determination to truly enjoy the festive season this year; to make sure that everything goes off okay this time, and that there are no disasters. Each time, however, there are stresses, fights, calamitous misunderstandings, just as there always are in real life at this time of year.

Of the eleven Christmas episodes it's hard to choose a single favourite. The boxed set of the complete series is a thing of joy and, every couple of years, we cycle back through the whole thing, all over again. When it comes to Christmas, somewhere in the middle of the series' long run is probably best – when the cast and writing team are at their height and it seemed like they couldn't put a foot wrong.

So – I could choose the episode in which Frasier has to pretend his entire family is Jewish, in order to impress his new girlfriend's mother, or the one in which he throws a party and no one turns up, and Daphne learns at last about Niles' six year-long crush on her. I think I'll go for the episode from season five, *Perspectives on Christmas*, which is rich with beautiful character moments – that touching sweetness under the bluster and pretension – and the sheer silliness and farce that the series frequently indulged in. So that, while at one moment we have this lovely, sophisticated idea of running scenes again from different characters' point of view as an exercise in perception, there are also plenty of moments that are just absurdly silly for the sake of it – such as Niles being stuck in the elevator with a Christmas tree.

Frasier is one of those shows in which you get to know all the regulars so well that it's like visiting friends. That's exactly the feeling you want to get from a Christmas episode, I think. As in any long-running show, however, they later messed around with the formula and the dynamics – dangerously, in pairing off Niles and Daphne. Somewhere in the middle it achieved a perfect balance, with Frasier himself at the height of his pomposity – here, hilariously trying to teach his father to sing, and Daphne at her glorious ditziest (before they tried to make her too sexy and self-aware).

One of my favourite characters was always the jaded, slightly slutty Roz, Frasier's number two at the radio station, and the tirade she performs here, while dressed as Mrs Claus in a department store grotto, is a joy to behold. Frasier has accidentally let slip to her mother the fact that Roz is going to be a single mother quite soon and on learning this Roz goes ballistic: practically beating up Santa in front of all the kids. I always thought that, given that the whole show ended with Roz suddenly becoming the head of the radio station, a sequel series with her at the helm would have been the next obvious move, but unfortunately, that never came to be.

Revisiting **Frasier** is like having the Nineties in a little box. How nice to go back and hang out with old pals, back before the Millennium.

The Good Life

Episode Title: Silly, but it's Fun

Channel: BBC 1

Original UK Transmission Date: 26 December 1977

Regular Cast: Felicity Kendal (Barbara Good), Richard Briers (Tom Good), Penelope Keith (Margo Leadbetter), Paul Eddington (Jerry Leadbetter)

Guest Cast: David Battley (Bill)

Writers: John Esmond, Bob Larbey

Director: John Howard Davies

When the Leadbetters' Christmas is cancelled by an irate Margo, Tom and Barbara save the day by inviting them over for a self-sufficient Christmas – total cost, 15 pence!!

One of the greatest seventies sit-coms reaches its very height in 1977, with one of the greatest episodes of anything ever made by the BBC. The work coming out of the studios at the heart of TV Centre in Shepherd's Bush in that period is astonishing to me. It's like looking back at MGM studios in the 1930s, when you can hardly credit the sheer volume of delightful nonsense they were churning out.

I believed in all four lead characters in **The Good Life**. Years after the show ended I dreamed about there being a sequel in which we find out what had happened to them all, down in well-heeled, complacent Surbiton, through all the upheavals of the Thatcher years and the strange revolutions in taste that the Nineties brought. Had Tom and Barbara's experiments in self-sufficiency worked out in the end? Had they survived, living off homegrown produce and wearing homespun clothes? And what about the snobby but lovable Margo and Jerry next door? Their callow, cultureless, tasteless posturing was very much in tune with the coming age. Thatcher's era would have rewarded the Leadbetters very well.

But the rise of Green politics and the increasing public awareness of ecological issues and alternative lifestyles might have wrought interesting changes on all four of them. I used to wonder – what if their positions changed? What if, in later life, Margo became a trendy eco-warrior? And what if Barbara was forced to go back into the workforce while Tom fiddled with his compost, and she kept the wolves from the door by donning a Nineties power suit?

Back in the seventies they are living in a more innocent, carefree age. The era of ABBA: that other foursome trapped in time; another foursome spiced with a gentle savour of wife-swapping.

I think kids of that era loved **The Good Life** then and into adulthood because – more than any other show – it showed grown-ups behaving as grown-ups. Unlike kids' TV, which was always embarrassing when adults tried to carry on like children, in **The Good Life** the characters lived properly adult lives, but because they were childless, when they carried on childishly, it wasn't to patronize the kids. They did it because they enjoyed it. These were grown-ups on their own, behaving how they would, and to kids this is enthralling. At Christmas the temptation to be silly is heightened and we see the Goods and Leadbetters getting dizzy on home-brewed peapod wine and playing silly games, getting hot and sticky dashing about. They also flirt good-naturedly and have a few deliciously tense moments when truths get told.

There are some wonderful truth-telling moments in this show. It's Margo who gets the greatest lines here. The episode begins with her cancelling Christmas outright, because she's foolishly messed up her order with Harrods. Fearing social shame, she calls off the whole shebang – much to genial husband Jerry's bleary, exhausted bemusement. But they are both rescued by Tom and Barbara, bearing homemade gifts and crackers. They bring them into their Christmas next door – a cheap and wholesome one, with real food that 'tastes like food' and games that are childlike and silly, as they ought to be.

Margo learns a lot about her own pretentiousness and snobbery. After Tom gives her a talking to in the kitchen – 'Listen, you!' – she joins in with gusto. Such is the charm of the writing and the performances none of it feels heavy-handed or preachy. It just feels like fun.

They behave with raucous decorum and everyone gets along just fine. It's a suburban Utopian ideal and that's what this show was always about. Parochial, middle class and even a little twee, perhaps, but it was filled with effortless charm and goodwill. It asked the big question that great literature always asks: 'But how should we live?'

And it was always just the right side of racy for its jokes to be eternally funny. The line about the oo-ah bird laying square eggs will be hilarious forever. But funnier is Margo's disappointment at not understanding, and even funnier again are the other three, falling about laughing at her polite dismay.

He Man and She-Ra

Episode Title: A Christmas Special

Channel: ITV

Original UK Transmission Dates: 30 December 1985

Regular Cast: John Erwin (He Man / Prince Adam), Alan Oppenheimer (Skeletor, Man-At-Arms), Linda Gary (Teela / Queen Marlena), Melendy Britt (She-Ra / Princess Adora)

Guest Cast: George DiCenzo (Hordak), Erika Scheimer (Peekablue / Perfuma), R.D Robb (Miguel)

Writers: Don Heckman, Bob Forward

Directors: Bill Reed, Ernie Schmidt

Orko accidentally gets beamed to Earth during a test of a new spy satellite. And when he returns he brings two Earth children, Alisha and Manuel, along with him. Filled with Christmas spirit, the children attract the attention of Skeletor.

A glorious team-up spectacular, with the entire casts of two mighty Filmation shows of the Eighties coming together to have a Christmas party. The denizens of Etheria have decamped to Eternia and when we first see them they're all trimming up Castle Grayskull in festive colours. The Queen is telling the King all about Christmas traditions on Earth (she's like Spock's mum, I guess?) and we get reminded that He Man and She-Ra are siblings who live in separate realms, having their own separate adventures and bad guys. But at Christmas the whole clan gets together.

She-Ra has brought all of her friends with her and, it must be said, her gang of butterfly people, unicorns, witches and men with moustaches is even more gay-looking than He Man's entourage of muscle-bound mincers. Castle Grayskull is *screaming* this season, and they seem set to have themselves a ball.

The story – such as it is – involves Orko, the irksome, legless sprite, messing up and transporting two human children into Eternia. He also brings about the temporary rehabilitation of that blue meanie, Skeletor. If you recall, He Man's ultimate nemesis was a hugely muscular, skull-faced queen who had a horde of mutants at his beck and call. Here, he's forced to play nursemaid to the lost human children and, gradually, he finds himself becoming sympathetic and – to his eternal shame – even rather nice.

When one of the children passes out in the snow, Skeletor actually takes pity and uses his dark, evil magic to summon up anoraks.

Take a moment to appreciate that. Skeletor uses his dark, evil magic to create anoraks.

The children try to explain Christmas to him.

It's when people have fun.

'You mean they get into fights?' asks Skeletor hopefully.

They shake their heads. 'It's when they give gifts.'

Skeletor asks, 'Gifts that explode?'

The kids realise that he isn't really evil. He's just thin-skinned.

Later, when Skeletor lies unconscious, the cute robot dog, Relay, licks his face until he wakes. This seems to touch the cosmic villain's heart, as if he realizes that he can be loved by a dog, too. (However, if you think about it, and if he'd taken a moment longer to think about it, it's quite obvious why that little dog was licking Skeletor's face. It's made out of bone. That's not fondness. The dog was peckish.)

'I don't like to feel good! I like to feel evil!' protests the quintessence of wickedness as the party goes on around him. He Man and She-Ra and all their colorful friends chuckle at his predicament, knowing that he will be back to his usual self soon enough.

The most evil thing in this whole animated special turns out to be the sappy song, halfway through, about peace and love and understanding. It's truly nasty.

K9 and Company

Episode Title: A Girl's Best Friend

Channel: BBC 1

Original UK Transmission Date: 28 December 1981

Regular Cast: Elisabeth Sladen (Sarah Jane Smith), John Leeson (Voice of K9)

Guest Cast: Colin Jeavons (George Tracy), Bill Fraser (Bill Pollock), Nigel Gregory (Vince Wilson), Sean Chapman (Peter Tracy), Mary Wimbush (Aunt Lavinia), Ian Sears (Brendan Richards), Linda Polan (Juno Baker), Neville Barber (Howard Baker), John Quarmby (Henry Tobias), Gillian Martell (Lily Gregson), Stephen Oxley (P.C. Carter)

Writer: Terence Dudley

Director: John Black

The Doctor has returned Sarah Jane Smith to Earth, where she has rebuilt her journalistic career and has come to pay her Aunt Lavinia a Christmas visit in the English village of Moreton Harwood. However, Aunt Lavinia is gone, and nobody knows where she is, though local rumour has it that she has fallen victim to a local witch coven.

It was the first spin-off from **Doctor Who** and so it was the first chance fans got to see that the universe continued to happen in places where the Doctor wasn't. This was our confirmation that things went on after he left and before he returned to present day Earth. People like Sarah Jane Smith, who had whizzed through adventures with him for several years, carried on living, having further adventures of their own. It seems obvious now – after years of expanded universe tie-in media, spin-offs, and team-ups of every kind – but all of this was novel in 1981. **Doctor Who** was a narrative that followed only Doctor Who. If he wasn't on-screen, then he was surely on his way. We assumed that everywhere he *wasn't* in the universe wasn't much worth watching.

When **K9 and Company** was first broadcast it was right in the gap between the reigns of the Fourth and Fifth Doctors. We were on a cliffhanger with a fresh new Doctor sitting bewildered in a field, wearing the clothes of his old self. We were avid for the next instalment in the new year, but first there was this Christmas side-step. A very welcome interruption in the shape of old friends meeting: a shaggy dog's tale indeed.

K9 and Company's pilot (indeed, only) episode is something I find difficult to encapsulate quickly. I've watched it almost every Christmas Eve since it was first shown. I must love it a lot, while at the same time knowing – and I've always known – that it isn't actually all that good. It's a barely-functional mystery story. It has the most marvelously hideous theme tune and the lead actress seems cross rather than chuffed to be starring in a solo adventure.

Why do I remember Lis Sladen's Sarah Jane Smith being wonderfully upbeat and happy all the time? She took travel through time and space in her stride. She was glamorous and sweet and ready to fight the good fight whether she was on Skaro, Peladon or Nerva Beacon. Why is it that when I go back and watch, it seems like she's complaining all the time, and looking piqued? **K9 and Company** she spends being quietly furious at a thousand inconveniences. Her aunt has annoyingly vanished. She's been awkwardly landed with a gawky nephew to look after. The house is cold and there are 'gypsy-looking' types hanging around. And what's this irritating packing case cluttering up Aunt Lavinia's sitting room? Christ, it's a robot dog. What do I want with one of those? Sarah stomps about in a range of mohair pullovers, capes and jumpsuits in autumnal shades, looking miffed. She tosses her crimped early Eighties hairdo in frustration and curses her various predicaments.

To be fair, Sarah's recently been living the life of a glamorous journalist, jetting all over the world and filing copy for Reuters. Her craggy old aunt filled us in at the start: Sarah Jane can never stay still in one place for very long. A whole Christmas at the shabby, stately old pile known as Moreton Harwood seems like torture to Ms. Smith. All this talk of market gardening and village gossip is anathema to her. She perks up a bit when she hears that certain of the neighbours might be practicing Satanists. This sounds promising.

Soon she and her irksome nephew and K9 are busy investigating. It's all to do with soil analysis, swarthy men creeping around in the dark, and awkward teatime chatter with the politely sinister post-mistress. For the first adventure of this proposed new series it seems we are no longer in a science fiction show: we're in the world of Enid Blyton.

What's marvelous is that it's Enid Blyton via Dennis Wheatley and **The Devil Rides Out**, for these very villagers who were so opposed to the use of science in market gardening really are worshippers of Beelzebub. They're planning human sacrifices at Samhain in a chilly graveyard. Guessing which of the villagers are the evil ones is thrilling stuff and my favourite moments all come not from the clumsily-handled revelations, but the red herrings thrown in our way. My favourite red herring of all is the voluptuous, hermaphroditic figure of Juno Baker – the confidante of Aunt Lavinia. She has a sly-looking husband and a constant sherry party going on in her cottage. She seems very keen to inculcate Sarah Jane into some form of naughtiness. As an audience we assume this means witchcrafty goings-on, and we're amazed to find she and her husband are nothing of the sort. They're probably only swingers.

Juno Baker with her shock of brown curly hair, her penchant for burgundy satin and lounging around, enunciating every line like Tim Curry in **The Rocky Horror Picture Show** – how I longed for her to turn out to be a surprise cameo from Tom Baker in drag. How wonderfully shocking that would have been on the Christmas Eve following his fictional demise.

I can't justify this rationally, but I love every moment of this silly drama. It's inept as mystery, and as horror and as adventure. It's a reunion for two characters who never met. Everyone mills around and no one is quite sure how sinister they should or shouldn't be. The final punch-up during the midnight sabbat in the graveyard is hilarious, with Sarah Jane doing judo in green wellies and K9 happily blasting all and sundry with his dear little nose laser.

I love it all to bits and nothing – no single episode of any **Doctor Who** spin-off (even those also featuring Sarah Jane and K9) – will ever replace it in my affections.

Larry Grayson's Generation Game

> **Episode Title**: New Year's Show
>
> **Channel**: BBC 1
>
> **Original UK Transmission Date**: 3 January 1982
>
> **Regular Cast**: Larry Grayson (Host), Isla St Clair (Hostess)
>
> **Producers:** Marcus Plantin, Keith Stewart

I'm watching the very last show they did. It's one of their annual round-ups of highlights and outtakes. Larry sits like a benign Roman Emperor with his Scottish concubine, surrounded by children (mostly from Nepal, it seems) and he announces – rather like Ziggy Stardust – that this is the last show they'll ever do. He tells us all that we shouldn't be sad. 'Let's go out singing! Like we always did!'

The choice of song – the Carpenters' 'Sing' – is exactly right, I think, fitting the ethos of the show perfectly. That line about not worrying if your best attempt at singing isn't good enough for anyone else to listen to – it's essential to the gentle game show Larry presided over for those four years. The song tells us: even if you're rubbish, you still have to sing your own tune.

Between 1978 and 1982 **The Generation Game** encouraged hordes of ordinary people, in mismatched, cross-generational pairs, to make an absolute show of themselves. They marched, they rolled out pastry, guessed mystery smells, did magic tricks and performed strange and intricate dances. The accent in those years was always on the audience laughing *with* the contestants, rather than at them. This was helped along by the gentle self-mockery of Larry Grayson himself, who would always place himself in the firing line first. The visitors to his show received very careful handling, I think – at least, compared with the earlier and later incarnations of the same show which were hosted by Bruce Forsyth. Brucie was always far more keen on outshining everyone, and proving that he was the best singer and dancer and comedian. He liked to make sure everyone knew what a wonder he was, and then he would set about making the contestants look complete fools. It's quite a different show in Larry and Isla's hands, I think.

Looking back at this ancient era, when I was between eight and twelve, it's amazing to see how brazen the camp humour is. Larry has some wonderful moments of – while never quite being out or outed – a gorgeous kind of flaunting of his gayness before the prime time Saturday evening audience. There's something virginal and prim about him the whole time, but he often refers to his offscreen chums – Slack Alice and Everard. He has a pantheon of racy imaginary friends, and it is they who get the blame for his occasional blue-tinged epithets.

His fondness for his assistant Isla, and vice versa, is very plain to see. This was an era of skimpily-clad women who stood around pointing at prizes and having very little to say for themselves. Larry is very keen that everyone admires Isla for her actual talents – she sings, she talks to camera, she expresses her own opinions, she gets the giggles when he sends her up. They even show a clip of her forthcoming solo show about farming.

The earlier compilation show comes from New Year's Eve 1979, when they tell us, we're all preparing to say goodbye to the Seventies and preparing ourselves for the Eighties. For this show we get to sit in the more intimate and cosy confines behind Larry's special door, at stage right. Through the series this is the door his surprise guests get to enter from, and we've never been privy to what supposedly lies beyond. It turns out to be a comfy sitting room, all decked out for Christmas, with a roaring fire, and an old wooden-sided telly.

It's rather like climbing aboard Larry Grayson's very own TARDIS for this episode.

I suppose he had a magic door because of his famous catchphrase of the time, 'Shut that door!'

He would pronounce it with a toss of the head and a backward kick of one leg. The audience roared each time, as they always do with catchphrases, without ever wholly understanding what they mean.

There are two possible sources for Larry's phrase. Both are steeped in hidden Queer history. One version is about the semi-legalisation of sex between men in 1967: i.e. such things were legal, so long as they occurred between consenting adults behind closed doors. Legally, there couldn't even be anybody else in the same building. An obvious absurdity, and one celebrated in this phrase. Shut that door: let's pretend we're alone and in the clear.

The other version dates back earlier, when relations between gay men were even more iffy and dodgy. Miming 'shut that door' across a room is a covert way of announcing 'Je t'adore'. Try it out!

These compilations are priceless. He sits weeping with laughter on his settee at what a fool he's made of himself. It's like being able to look at yourself and your family and friends at all kinds of parties in the past. He flubs his lines, he interrupts, he gets it wrong – and he just doesn't care. He couldn't give two hoots about being perfect and slick. He's just funny and while he's up on stage, his audience adores him.

I love the story – apparently true – that after each show his driver would come and fetch him in the Rolls Royce and he'd eat fish and chips out of the paper as they drove all the way north to Nuneaton, where he lived alone in a bungalow.

The Morecambe and Wise Show

Episode Title: 1975 Christmas Show

Channel: BBC 1

Original UK Transmission Date: 25 December 1975

Regular Cast: Eric Morecambe (Himself), Ernie Wise (Himself)

Guest Cast: Diana Rigg (Herself), Des O'Connor (Himself), Gordon Jackson (Butler), Robin Day (Himself), Diane Solomon (Herself), Brenda Arnau (Herself), Ann Hamilton (Shopkeeper), Pan's People (Themselves), Debbie Ash (Des O'Connor Fan), Fiona Gray (Des O'Connor Fan)

Writers: Eddie Braben (additional material by Eric Morecambe and Ernie Wise)

Producer: Ernest Maxin

Eric and Ernie give each other Christmas presents, and Des O'Connor gets revenge on the pair.

Theirs are the first shows mentioned when anyone talks about British TV at Christmas. For all those years between 1968 and 1977 they were a staple feature of festive viewing. They were well-nigh sacrosanct. The shows became more lavish, the dance numbers more elaborate, the stars starrier and, at their height, Morecambe and Wise were getting more people to watch their old-fashioned Variety show than anyone had ever watched anything.

Certain images are burned into the nation's consciousness. Shirley Bassey in an evening gown and one workman's boot. Solemn newsreaders decked out as sailors doing gymnastics in a **South Pacific** spoof. Eric's soaked policeman during 'Singing in the Rain.' I expect elements of these sketches are answers in some bogus governmental 'Good British Citizen' test.

The thing that always intrigues me about **Morecambe and Wise** is how shabby it always looks. They must have spent a lot of money on it, but it still seems rather thrown together and decidedly un-glamorous. The floor of their white stage where they do their final number always looks a bit mucky. Partly this is a result of being a Seventies kid grown up, looking back at the time when adults sweated in terrible polyester clothes and smoked fags constantly – a time before rigorous grooming.

There is also, in **Morecambe and Wise**, a deliberate feeling of it all being slightly amateur and invented on the spot. This is the story of these shows, in fact, with them scrabbling to find guests to appear and doing everything at the last minute; it's one of their enduring jokes. The audience loved their corpsing and giggling and their adlibs, and their guest stars being put off their stroke. It's well-documented, though, just how much careful effort went into the off-the-cuffness of these shows. But I still think the glint in Eric Morecambe's eye represents real danger and real mischief. We know that the guests know that he can throw a spanner into the works at any given moment and bring down the entire house. All he needs to give is a word, a twitch, a sly sideways look. His is the kind of rare presence that is hilarious without his having to do much of anything at all. He's funny before he even opens his mouth.

In these shows they practically invented that genre of TV in which film and pop stars send themselves up, sacrificing what dignity they had for the sake of the show, and proving what a great sport they are. It's a very British tradition, I think, that not only can we not respect, nor even like, someone until we have seen them make a complete fool of themselves on TV. Only then will we consider letting them into our hearts. Angela Ripon is loved by the nation not for enunciating words at a desk in a posh voice, but for the bit when her desk slid away and she started doing high kicks with Eric and Ernie.

For myself, I don't think all their sketches are as funny as those of their main rivals in the late Seventies, **The Two Ronnies**. I don't think all their shows hold up as well as we always assume, all these years later. I think we've probably seen them too much

– repeated, repackaged, regurgitated every Christmas since they stopped producing them. They can sometimes feel a bit like turkey curry three days after Boxing Day. They belong to a part of the past that seems as irrecoverable and gone as the Edwardian era to us now. They're so canonised and revered it's hard to appreciate, sometimes, their gleeful anarchy. We are inured to their sheer silliness and we must remember how deeply silly and enjoyable they were – back in their somewhat sexist, racist, homophobic, slightly smelly era. We must remember how deeply funny it was to that audience that these men were sitting up in bed together, so blithely, on Christmas Day 1975.

It's what some might call a more innocent age: the kind of time that old people might want to go back to, like they used to want to go back to the war. Times of certainty, when you knew who the enemy was, and you knew what the pecking order was, and everyone laughed at the same kind of things. Perhaps this is partly what Brexit is all about – the fond, nostalgic dreams of slightly dim people who earnestly wish we didn't live in a world of political-correctness-gone-mad. If only, they think, we could go back to the off-colour jokes of a different age...

It's worth mentioning that the BBC made a very nice TV movie in 2011 called **Eric and Ernie**. Usually their showbiz biopics are miserable affairs. There has been a vogue in recent years for plays in which we are exposed to the unfortunate lives of the stars who used to make us laugh. Very few of them are worth watching, but this one is fond and warm and beautifully made. Plus, Eric's mum and dad are played by Victoria Wood and Vic Reeves, which is just about perfect as casting gets.

Omnibus

Episode Title: Whistle and I'll Come to You

Original UK Transmission Date: 7 May 1968

Cast: Michael Hordern (Professor Parkins), Ambrose Coghill (Colonel), George Woodbridge (Hotel proprietor), Nora Gordon (Proprietress), Freda Dowie (Maid)

Writer: Jonathan Miller, adapted from M.R. James ('Oh, Whistle, and I'll Come to You, My Lad')

Director: Jonathan Miller

A university professor, confident that everything can be explained rationally, struggles to retain that belief on a holiday to a remote coastal village. After blowing on an ancient whistle that he discovered on the beach, strange and terrifying events overtake him.

Jonathan Miller's short black and white film of this ghost story is the first of the BBC's Christmas adaptations of M.R. James. Later they would be longer, and in colour, and they'd throw tales by Charles Dickens and Sheridan LeFanu into the mix, but they would remain terrifying throughout the seventies. Typically, they are subdued, gloomy, slow-moving... and then filled with sudden, shocking moments you didn't see coming.

This first one is this best in my book, not least because I think it's the best of James' stories, and also because it features Michael Hordern as the fusty old academic who comes to spend some time by the seaside, getting scared out of his wits. Hordern was the voice of Paddington Bear in the late seventies TV show and that was how I first came to know and love his voice. Later he was a mellifluous Gandalf in Radio 4's wonderful **Lord of the Rings**. His voice sounds like crumbling blue cheese: slightly crusty and sweet at the same time. In this play he gets to mumble and croon and pant and screech.

As with all other horror stories on film, the sound effects are the key to scaring the hell out of the viewer. What they do so brilliantly here is strip James' story of all of its ornate language – his beautiful syntax and academic vocabulary – and give us a soundtrack that is mostly very quiet. We have an empty beach and a guest house full of hush. Aproned woman go about their daily tasks. The quiet, we feel, is what this man is after. He and other men like him are seeking quiet getaways in which they can potter about, taking sandwiches with them to sit in the marram grass, peering into their books.

Hordern's little noises of appreciation and contemplation fill the soundtrack. We become attuned to them. He barely makes whole sentences, even when speaking to other characters. He is a man whose life is spent mostly inside his own mind. One of the nicest things here, though, is how he's presented as this intellectual, devoted to the life of the mind, but we are focused very much on his bodily noises – his grunts and eructations. There's a delicious bit when we see him slurping and clinking his way through breakfast, making short work of a soft boiled egg, all the while discussing the possibility of life after death with the man at the table opposite. We can hardly follow his words for all the noise of his eating.

While he chuckles and pooh-poohs the very idea of a haunting, Hordern is a marked man, and there are phantoms on his trail. Blithely he carries on enjoying his vacation, oblivious to everything... until his dreams start telling him that something spooky is going on. Every time he closes his eyes he's running down the shore being pursued by... something.

I remember first watching this play. It wasn't until BBC 4 started up and they had a series of wonderful repeats. Somehow I'd missed out on this show all my life. I don't think this series was repeated much. They were shown once, each Christmas. They flared up like fever dreams and then they were gone – back to the dusty archive.

The moment when we see the ghost on the beach was a real shock to me. It undulates on the spot like a twisting fragment of nightmare somehow caught on film. At first you're not quite sure you saw it. Then you blink and think: could it even be real? How on earth did they do it?

On a second viewing you can see how they accomplished the visual trick. On a third viewing it seems impossible that the shot holds the image in focus for so long. And you feel all over again... what is this ghastly thing we're being asked to stare at?

It's one of the most horrifying images in any horror story ever, I think. And yet... what is it? A dark will-o'-the-wisp. A shred of dark brilliance.

On later viewings it looks rather like an old bin bag being blown down the beach.

The film's suggestive mood has worked on us. In just a few moments we have been mesmerised and we will believe anything. By the final scene, when the bedclothes apparently come to life and start rising up of their own accord, we are ready to start squealing as loudly as Hordern himself. The events of the story reduce him to a gibbering, thumb-sucking basket case and we aren't far behind.

It's a story about a man who resolutely believes himself to be alone, even when he is with other people. His logic and intellect set him aside and he knows he is right about anything he puts his mind to. And yet it takes but half an hour to drive him completely out of his mind...

There's not the slightest thing Christmassy about any of this.

And yet Christmas Eve would be very much poorer without another repeat viewing of Michael Hordern's descent into raving madness.

Hordern also made an excellent Scrooge in the BBC's **Christmas Carol** of 1997: another very faithful piece of adaptation. Rather daringly the BBC remade **Whistle** in 2010 with John Hurt. They gave themselves a freer hand in transforming the material, adding an intriguing Alzheimers twist and a wife in the background. I quite liked it, though I did add it to the list of those adaptations that play fast and loose with the classics – with Arthur Conan Doyle, Henry James, etc, as well as M.R James.

The thing about remakes is that they seem like they are trying to supplant the original, but they hardly ever do. The original can always come back to haunt us...

Sherlock Holmes

Episode Title: The Blue Carbuncle

Channel: BBC 1

Original UK Transmission Date: 23 December 1968

Regular Cast: Peter Cushing (Sherlock Holmes), Nigel Stock (Doctor Watson)

Guest Cast: Madge Ryan (Lady Morcar), James Beck (James Ryder), Richard Butler (Harold Baker), Michael Robbins (Breckinridge), Frank Middlemass (Peterson), Ernest Hare (Windigate), Neil Fitzpatrick (Horner), Clyde Pollitt (Police Sergeant), Grace Arnold (Mrs. Hudson), Edna Doré (Mrs. Oakshott), Diana Chappell (Catherine Cusack)

Writer: Stanley Miller, adapted from Sir Arthur Conan Doyle

Director: Bill Bain

A precious gem goes missing from a luxury hotel, while Holmes is given a goose with an unusual meal in its stomach.

I dithered slightly over which version. One is from the Eighties and stars Jeremy Brett. It's one of those lavish **Sherlock** adaptations Granada made. Brett is an absolute hoot in this frivolous Christmas romp. It's astonishing to see how he camps and whoops it up. Often you remember the glowering tortured

Holmes he created on screen, and the funny one fades away slightly. He's clearly having a ball, making this episode.

The other choice – and probably my favourite, all things considered – is the 1968 BBC version starring Peter Cushing. It's cosy and studio-bound and feels just right. Cushing is a wonderfully bony, chiseled, intellectually alert Holmes. His courteousness and polite disengagement slips only once, at the very end, when the felon tries to thank him for his lenience and mercy and Cushing, rather startlingly, yells at him.

Both versions are properly, respectfully, faithful to the original story. It's a perfect puzzle box by Arthur Conan Doyle, this slightly daft tale of the goose club and the stolen jewel. Every little part of it works beautifully, I think – Holmes tricking everyone, dodging lightly ahead and doing it all effortlessly. Why *wouldn't* you film this or the other Holmes stories faithfully? Anything else seems an outrage when it comes to detective tales that unfold as beautifully as this.

Something about **Sherlock Holmes** at Christmas feels just right – conjuring the Victorian Christmases of our collective unconsciousness and introducing just the tiniest note of danger and excitement. This re-viewing reminded me that the villain in 1968 is that wonderful actor, James Beck, who played the spiv,

Private Walker, in **Dad's Army**. Here he gets a few minutes to whine connivingly and, like everyone else in this piece, judges it just right and makes it look easy.

I'd become rather jaded with Sherlockania in recent times. A surfeit of Holmes, perhaps, in his various forms. It's easy to lose a sense of what it is you love about a show or a fictional character. This fifty year old piece of slightly creaky TV worked wonders, making me fall in love with this world all over again.

The Lion, the Witch and the Wardrobe

Movie Title: The Lion, the Witch and the Wardrobe

Channel: ITV

Original UK Transmission Date: 1 April 1979

Regular Cast: Rachel Warren (Lucy), Susan Sokol (Susan), Reg Williams (Peter), Simon Adams (Edmund)

Guest Cast: Victor Spinetti (Mr. Tumnus), Dick Vosburgh (Professor), Don Parker (Mr. Beaver), Liz Proud (Mrs. Beaver), Stephen Thorne (Aslan), Nicholas Barnes (Edmund), Beth Porter and Sheila Hancock (Jadis – The White Witch), Arthur Lowe (Mr. Beaver), June Whitfield (Mrs. Beaver), Leo McKern (Professor), Leslie Phillips (Mr. Tumnus)

Writers: David D Connell, Bill Melendez adapted from C.S. Lewis

Director: Bill Melendez

Four children, Peter, Susan, Edmund and Lucy, enter the magical world of Narnia - a land of talking animals and mystical creatures – via a seemingly mundane wardrobe. Once there, they join forces with the noble lion Aslan in battle against the evil White Witch.

There are several adaptations of this classic novel and I've got things to say about almost all of them. Firstly, I have to point out

96

how very Christmassy C.S. Lewis's best book about Narnia is, in and of itself in the first place. His fantasy land is the quintessence of winter wonderlands, but it's also the place where it's 'always winter and never Christmas.' Somehow that very phrase cleverly conjures the sensation of being a kid in what used to be the endless lead-up to Christmas Day. At that age you feel like the days can't move fast enough... and so they creep along with wicked slowness.

For me, Lewis' frozen woodlands and the glimpses of fauns under street lamps, and witches dispensing Turkish Delight to naughty boys is the very essence of fantastic Christmas tale-telling. I wonder if it was the Christmas term at school when we first had this book read to us? I feel like it must have been. The **Narnia** books – along with other significant Puffins – were all read aloud to us at my junior school in the Seventies. They were books that we shared in spellbound company.

The first version I ever saw on TV is still my favourite: a 1979 cartoon, made by the people who made the Charlie Brown animated specials. In some ways it's the most basic version. It's short and sweet and almost minimalist in its execution. The figures are simply drawn. Just a few lines. Rudimentary figures. The style seems naïve at times when compared, say, with Disney or Don Bluth productions of the same era. I think that there's an elegance to the drawing, however. When you look at these representations of the White Witch or Aslan they seem very easy to draw. They invite and encourage the young audience to re-draw the characters and the scenes for themselves, afterwards. (I was forever following up the things I read and watched with further adventures and episodes committed to paper...)

It's a curious adaptation because it folds the story's opening up, beginning with Lucy's return from her first trip through the wardrobe into Narnia. It eschews all the gradual build-up and begins with her trying to convince everyone that the fantasy is real. Also, the film drops any attempt to place the story back in the War years. The children are no longer refugees. They're just Seventies kids in bright clothes and flares, visiting a funny old man in his big house in the country.

Like many simply-animated cartoons of the era it has the screen fizzing and shimmering because of its roughly hand-coloured quality. As in **Roobarb and Custard** or **The Mr Men** the scratchy, uneven hotness of felt tip colours set the characters quivering, giving them a vitality that a slicker, smoother style of animation can find hard to match. The snow falls skittishly and messily in almost every scene.

Another wonderful aspect of this version is the work of the voice artists. There has never been a better White Witch than Sheila Hancock. She is the shrieking embodiment of evil. Neurotic and nasty, her voice doing all kinds of gymnastics, perfectly fitting that bendy, pliable, manic queen heaped with furs and livid with facial contortions. Stephen Thorne as Aslan and Arthur Lowe and June Whitfield as Mr and Mrs Beaver are voices so familiar that you feel like you've known them forever. How could these characters ever sound like anyone else?[2]

So, what of the other versions? The 1988 BBC TV six part serial is worth watching because it is one of the very last of those nicely old-fashioned shows, in which the effects seem slightly homemade, but the costumes are dazzling and the acting somewhat camp. It's a respectful and reasonably sumptuous version in which the child actors are, as in so many BBC things, just like tiny old people in midget form, braying 1950s dialogue and stomping mulishly about. Perhaps there's a little too much reverence about this version, though? The BBC were setting off on a never-completed cycle of Narnias, and in the following years we had such delights at Tom Baker's hungover-seeming Puddleglum the Marsh Wiggle to look forward to. The

---

[2] The entire cast – with the exception of Stephen Thorne as Aslan – was different for the US version of the cartoon.

watchword was fidelity to the original and perhaps they miss out on the absurdity and the fun of the books?

The 2005 movie version is CGI heavy and overlong – a common fault in many post-millennial movies, of course. Characterisation and story-telling get swamped in the remorseless drive toward spectacle. The war between the evil hordes of the Witch and Aslan's army of mythical beasts is presented in all its glory, and for once we have a lovely sense of scale in Narnia. It actually feels as big as Middle Earth. But we also have the strange sight of the children actually engaging in battle, stabbing and slashing at the creatures. The thing about advances in film technology is that everything has become terribly literal. Hardly anything at all is left to the imagination. Someone else gets to do all the imagining for us and with stories like Lewis's this seems wrong to me.

A drama should only give us a hint of the strange and exotic world beyond. A faun pausing under street lamp in the snow, say. And we should be tantalised into picturing the rest for ourselves. An army of fauns attacking an army of witches and goblins soon gets tiring to watch and that's how I would describe this 2005 effort. It's just too much Lion, too much Witch and a tad too much Wardrobe.

I must make mention of another version, from the late Sixties. Only a couple of fragments seem to exist of this production, and they turned up on You Tube a couple of years ago. Both the excerpts came from a late episode, when the Witch goes to visit Aslan under truce, and makes her demands. It's startling to see the very theatrical way TV was produced back then. Rather than being an actual lion, Aslan is presented as a man on two legs in a leotard and animal mask. The same is true of the other animals in his court. He struts around quite freely as he engages in hostilities with the White Witch and all the focus is on the actors' performances. Effects are kept to a minimum, and there is live drumming and elements of dance as the characters weave about the set and taunt each other. This is a thrilling handful of moments and I wish there was more available.

Lastly, though it doesn't fit within the remit of this book, I'd like to put in a word for Radio Four's version of the tale, adapted by Brian Sibley in the early Nineties. It's concise, funny and charming, and it somehow retains the wit.

One thing that the various versions of Narnia have in common is wonderful music. They all have separate, quite different themes and soundtracks and all are fabulously evocative and nostalgic. Their job is to remind you of a place you are heartsick and homesick for: a place you only can only half-remember visiting.

Perhaps a land you haven't even been to yet. Each version has a tune that manages to encapsulate that feeling... with, again, the 1979 cartoon and its music by Michael J Lewis coming out on top.

A Muppet Family Christmas

Movie Title: A Muppet Family Christmas

Channel: BBC 1

Original UK Transmission Date: 26 December 1989

Cast: Frank Oz (Fozzie Bear / Animal / Miss Piggy / Bert / Grover / Cookie Monster / Sam the Eagle), Dave Goelz (The Great Gonzo / Dr. Bunsen Honeydew / Boober Fraggle / Zoot / Beauregard), Richard Hunt (Scooter / Janice / Statler / Beaker / Gladys the Cow / Two-Headed Monster / Snowman), Kathryn Mullen (Mokey Fraggle), Jerry Nelson (Emily 'Ma' Bear / Robin the Frog / Sgt. Floyd Pepper / Count von Count / Herry Monster / Two-Headed Monster / Gobo Fraggle / Camilla the Chicken), Karen Prell (Red Fraggle / Maureen the Mink), Steve Whitmire (Turkey / Rizzo the Rat / Wembley Fraggle / Sprocket the Dog / Lips), David Rudman (Miss Piggy's Photographer), Jim Henson (Kermit the Frog / Rowlf the Dog / Dr. Teeth / Swedish Chef / Waldorf / Ernie / Guy Smiley / The Newsman / Himself), Caroll Spinney (Big Bird / Oscar the Grouch), Gerard Parkes (Doc)

Writer: Jerry Juhl

Director: Peter Harris

Kermit and his friends pay a surprise Christmas visit to Fozzie Bear's mother's farm, where they are joined by all of Jim Hensons' other creations. But will Miss Piggy make it to the farm in time?

Others may choose **The Muppet Christmas Carol** and that film has great merit but this is a) my book, b) it's about telly and c) I prefer the Muppets when Jim Henson was still alive. I'm a Generation X purist when it comes to the Muppets. Absolutely hardcore. Anything after the end of the Eighties seems slightly inauthentic to me.

I know it's ridiculous to talk about inauthenticity when we're discussing creatures made of fake fur fabric with googly eyes, but what can I say? The Muppets are a serious business with me. There is something so life-affirming, anarchically funny, and deeply, endlessly creative about them. There's something incredibly touching about Henson's world and the characters he peopled it with. I've never tried to examine or analyse it: I've just always loved them, right from the day **The Muppet Show** was first broadcast in the UK in 1976. The cast appeared on the cover of that week's 'Look-In' comic. Just who *were* these strange creatures? Since then I've been a confirmed Muppet fan.

A Muppet Family Christmas is the very height of their accomplishment, I think. It's a bit like the **Dynasty** reunion, or the **Cagney and Lacey** TV movies, set well after their heyday, almost ten years later, after spin-offs and movies, they reunite for a TV special.

1987 was an amazing year for Henson devotees. We got David Bowie in **Labyrinth** and we got John Hurt in **The Storyteller** and we got this hour long special[3] in which Fozzie's mother's country cottage is descended upon by every Muppet there ever was. They get snowed in and everyone sings and does their party piece. It's hilarious and moving and everything you could ever want in a Christmas special.

Why, in my forties, do I find it so touching when the entire cast of **Sesame Street** turns up? Someone calls out and looks to the horizon and, coming through the wintry woods, caroling all the way, are the characters from that sister TV show. Big Bird comes lolloping through the fake fir trees.

Perhaps I over-identify with Henson's characters?

It's true that I go through life brimming with hope and trying to be friendly, and trusting that if I treat everyone like a friend that attitude will always come back at me. (A strategy doomed to failure, as I've been warned on many occasions – but it's never stopped me trying.) Also, I have a whole bunch of odd-looking friends (some of them furry). Also, as a person whose parents divorced when I was seven (the year I first saw **The Muppets**)

---

[3] First shown in the United States on 16 December 1987.

and as someone who is forever shuttling between warring family factions, always trying to make peace, I have an innate love of narratives which bring together separate groups of characters. Cameos, team-ups, surprise visits, cross-overs – they all get my vote. I love it when Kermit and his nephew go into the cellar, discover a hole in the wall and, beyond it, the entire world of the Fraggles. They spend the few moments of a song in that strange, parallel world, extolling the virtues of passing on gifts.

Everyone's on top form in this special. Poor Fozzie's mom (surely just Fozzie in glasses and a wig?) is hoping to get to Bermuda to avoid the bad weather; alarmed to find that her house has been invaded by her son's friends. The hilarious sub-plot of Miss Piggy's delayed arrival. Rolf's joyous appreciation of an out-of-tune piano. And the sassy turkey offering the Swedish Chef Big Bird as a viable alternative for Christmas dinner.

There's nothing about this parade of routines that isn't great (except maybe the home movie featuring **The Muppet Babies**. They were always a mistake).

After Miss Piggy's arrival and an extended singalong at the end there is a delightful cameo. Jim Henson himself is shown slaving away in the kitchen, doing all the washing up, working busily behind the scenes. He tells Sprocket, the dog from **Fraggle Rock**: 'I like it when they have a good time.'

And so do we.

The Real Christmas Show

Movie Title: The Real Christmas Show
Channel: Channel 4
Original UK Transmission Date: 24 December 1996
Cast: Gaby Roslin (Presenter)

How many times have you watched **The Real Christmas Show**? And what it is it about this programme that seems to mean you have to watch it at least once a year?

You taped it in 1996. It was a festive spin-off from a show about summer holidays[4]: one that purported to tell the truth about 'real' holidays by supplying members of the public with video cameras. They would film themselves behaving 'naturally' abroad and then the results would be shown as they watched themselves alongside a TV audience, and they'd be covered in embarrassment and shame. And so would we, because we'd somehow share their shame: recognising our own selves and our own typical holiday behaviour in all their goings-on.

---

[4] **The Real Holiday Show**, (1995-2000)

The Christmas show works in just the same way, with extra tinsel and sparkles and, because it's Christmas, with far more potential for embarrassment.

Ten years after this show was broadcast (and surely well after everyone had forgotten about it) I transferred it from VHS to a disc, because that was the year we first had one of those fancy DVD recorders and I spent many happy hours one Christmas digging through old tapes from the cellar and finding vintage gems hardly anyone would care about.

Now ten years more have passed and still I watch **The Real Christmas Show** each year.

It's completely ephemeral, and yet it was the very first show I ever chose to preserve in my idiosyncratic archive. It is the very definition of throwaway TV and perhaps that is why I feel so attached to it? I get the feeling that, if I don't preserve it, then no one will.

So, here are seven families recording themselves during Christmas 1995 – making home movies or what were called back then 'video diaries'. A year later they're in the studio, in the throes of a Christmas party in a winter wonderland. They sit at tables, all a bit tanked up on Christmas booze, watching each other's movies and getting interviewed by Gaby. It's a kind of cabaret show in which everyone is a star.

What really appeals to me here is the idea that everyone is given a chance to star in the movie of their lives. It bears out something I really believe: that the tiniest, most mundane moments in anybody's life are rife with intense drama and emotion. People doing just ordinary stuff is absolutely fascinating.

It's Christmas too, and the enormous pressure this puts people under is also completely fascinating.

It's amazing to think that these seven mini-narratives of seven very different families, all across the UK, are happening at exactly the same time, on the same day. It's a Mass Observation exercise, with a festive theme.

And me? I remember that Christmas well, too. I was in Edinburgh with a bunch of friends. We lived in our little flat in the centre of the city, high above the snowy streets (it snowed late that Christmas Day – as it does in all these seven little films.) I was in my mid-twenties and it was my first ever Christmas away from my family at home, and so it was a big deal. It was a time for remembering old family rituals and sharing other people's and inventing our own.

Many years later – 2009, I think – I was passing through John Lennon International Airport. I heard a loud, braying Scouse accent, followed by ricocheting volleys of laughter. I turned round, thinking I recognized that piercing voice from somewhere. I scanned the tables of the bar I was passing, thinking I'd see someone I knew. But I didn't know any of these people. When she laughed again, and I looked harder, I suddenly realized that the woman was the mother at the centre of the Liverpool family in 'The Real Christmas Show.' Here she was, with her best mate, fourteen years on from the recording of that show. To me it was like seeing someone famous from the telly. Her raucous, horrible laughter had been a carillon of bells through every Christmas Eve since the mid-Nineties for me. (I wonder if even she had watched the show as much as I had? I wondered if any of the participants had?) I wanted to go over and tell her: I love your work.

She's the one who, when her family members sing 'Why are we waiting?' as she puts finishing touches to Christmas lunch, says: 'I'm sharpening my knife so I can cut the throats of the lot of you.'

Each of the seven families in this show says or does something to make you fall in love with them. You want to be part of all their families, just for a little while.

There's the young couple in Cornwall. They have everyone back to theirs. They bicker and laugh with their big, boisterous family. She's rather ill, you can tell. She has less energy than the others. She can't run into the sea with her husband and his friends. They tell the story of how she's had a heart and lung transplant and her life has been transformed. But it won't last forever. They know that every Christmas they have here, in this lovely Cornish house, with all their loved ones around them, is intensely precious.

They're not mawkish or sentimental for a second. They're matter-of-fact and just lovely, and your heart melts.

More tricky is the dodgy stepfather and the hapless student, who turns up and knows he is hated by the rancid old drunk. They are visited by squawking, show-off American friends, who only make everything worse. It's toe-curling and excruciating and the video fizzes and blurs as it edits out the worst of the family rows. The mother tries to hold it all together, but she's hampered by the fact that she wants to please her husband first. It's uncomfortable viewing and, back in the studio, one year on, the old git is still drunk – and you can tell Gaby wants to tell him off. She barely restrains herself.

I'm fond, too, of the Newcastle family and the two women who stay up all night, working for a taxi firm. They open their presents on the dot of midnight and dance around with lit ciggies at three in the morning.

Then there's the lady in Norfolk who bedecks her house in thousands of Christmas lights. Or rather, her husband does. We learn all about the vastness of her Christmas preparations and how she can't leave even the toilet untrimmed by tinsel or lights. Her poor husband is up on the roof of their house sticking bulbs in sockets and spooling out wires. In her film she declares she might have something wrong with her: this compulsion is perhaps a bit obsessive. And then we get the news that her poor harried husband has had a stroke since last Christmas.

It comes as little surprise.

She has written a little poem about mortality and making the best of every year, which she intones at the end.

It's trite and it's embarrassing, but this show is more truly Christmassy than almost anything I've ever seen on TV. It's about the lengths we go to in order to make sure we're together and having a good time – and about the awkwardness of it all, when we do.

The Snowman

> **Movie Title:** The Snowman
> **Channel:** Channel 4
> **Original UK Transmission Date:** 26 December 1982
> **Cast:** David Bowie (Introduction / Older James)
> **Writer:** Raymond Briggs
> **Directors:** Dianne Jackson, Jimmy T Murakami

On Christmas Eve, a young boy builds a snowman that comes to life and takes him to the North Pole to meet Santa Claus.

This animated classic is the perfect Christmas Eve treat: nothing sets the mood better. It's also a lovely example of how to subvert that disappointing old cliché: 'I woke up and it was all a dream...'

It's a gentle tale, beginning small scale, with a boy dashing out on a snowy Christmas Eve to build his snowman. The animators' most brilliant achievement among many is in retaining the atmosphere of Raymond Briggs' pages: amplifying that feeling, somehow. He typically colours with layers of pencils, there are very few hard edges or outlines, and this gives his pictures a wonderful softness, and slightly misty feeling: a nostalgia that is never overly-sweet. Captured on film, his scenes are buzzing and quivering with life. Everything vibrates with colour. It feels very much like snow is falling continuously throughout the film and you get that dreamlike, floating sensation throughout: a perfect marriage of subject and style.

There was always something very magical about this cartoon. The flight to the North Pole is still breathtaking. I suppose these days the illusion would be a lot easier to accomplish, all that swooping about and vertiginous angles and forced perspectives. Back then I gather it was all done by hand and part of the piece's vitality comes from knowing that it's the work of many hands, scribbling away over many months. People drawing snowmen and conjuring snow through many seasons...

After a night of wild rumpus with all the other snowmen at their annual ball and even an appearance by Santa, it's time to return home for Christmas morning. And the ending brings the horrible revelation of a melted snowman – a tragic finish which never gets any easier. Then, in the final seconds before the credits roll, the boy reaches into his dressing gown pocket and finds the scarf he was given by Santa last night. It's still there. Blue and decorated with a snowman motif. And so it was all real. The boy stares at it in freeze frame at the very end and it's the perfect answer to the 'it was all a dream' school of fantasy (**Oz, Alice, The Box of Delights**... and the vague feeling of disappointment those endings always bring.)

A lovely – and I hope not wholly apocryphal – story about **The Snowman** involves the filmed introduction. The first year it was broadcast – 1982 and Channel Four's inaugural season – it was introduced by Raymond Briggs. For the first repeat showing, the following year, a new short prologue was filmed and this proved to be the enduring, classic version. It's the last piece of the jigsaw, making the whole thing perfect. It's David Bowie exploring the old junk and toys in an attic, talking to camera, remembering the events of the cartoon we're about to see.

'You see, it was a real snowman...'

He's there with his nicotine-blonde hair and it's hard to explain how other-worldly Bowie himself seemed to kids in those days. He was a creature from another decade, an alien future... and here he was telling us he was once the boy from the **Snowman** cartoon. That kid hurrying about, dragging his clothes on, keen to dash into the snow – he had a lifetime of stardom to look forward to. This ordinary little boy – would he one day be Ziggy Stardust? It was a funny thing to think.

The apocryphal story goes like this. There was a young woman working for the film company in Soho, the year they made **The Snowman**. She had a pretty lowly job in the office, but she could

117

knit. It was she who had created the scarf prop for the filmed scene in the attic. She had knitted it so it looked exactly like the one in the cartoon, so that Bowie could pick it up and remember his magical adventure.

When Bowie was visiting the offices of the company to toast the success of the film, there was a great buzz in the building. Everyone wanted to see him, but he was whisked straight up to the top floor to meet the men in suits. The people in the humbler offices below barely got a glimpse of him. After his meeting he was hustled right out again to his waiting limo and everyone was disappointed. The young woman and her colleagues were hanging out of their window, watching his car zigzag away through the Soho streets.

She felt a particular attachment to that film because of the scarf she had knitted for it. She'd worked hard to get it right. It was an important prop because it was the link between the everyday world and the world of magic.

On the day of Bowie's fleeting visit, this young woman had come into work with one of her boyfriend's favourite albums, 'Hunky Dory', on vinyl, in a brown paper bag. She'd carried it very carefully on the tube that morning, and she had set it on her desk while she got on with the day's work, excitedly waiting for the moment when the Thin White Duke would pass through the office and she could jump up and get it signed.

But he never came by.

It was just a flying visit.

At the end of the day she went home disconsolately and told her boyfriend that she'd had no luck. He didn't mind, but he wanted to know what she'd done with his favourite record. He'd had it since he was a kid.

'Oh, I must have left it on my desk,' she said. She had been so cheesed off about the whole business that she had forgotten it. 'I'll bring it home tomorrow, promise.'

The next day she had wiped the whole saga from her mind. She went into work, the same as any other day. Into Central London, into Soho, into the office. She sat herself down at her desk.

And there it was, right in front of her. Her boyfriend's beloved copy of 'Hunky Dory'. But there were black scribbles all over the cover picture; all over Bowie's soft focus beauty in black marker pen. It was signed with love, and dedicated to the girl who had knitted his scarf for him.

She sat staring at it for a while – at the lightning bolt of his signature – trying to figure out how he could have known. Also, how had he done it? She had seen him leave the building. She had hardly left her desk all day. He had no idea who she was...

She never found out the answer. Years later she was still telling the story and still trying to figure it out.

When Bowie died she told the story to one of the newspapers and that's how I heard it. It was my favourite story of all the ones flying about that week. It was a story about that snowman magic creeping wonderfully, mysteriously, into real life, making a Christmassy story in the bleakest part of the year.

The Story Lady

Movie Title: The Story Lady

Original US Transmission Date: 29 December 1991

Cast: Jessica Tandy (Grace McQueen), Stephanie Zimbalist (Julie Pollard), Lisa Jakub (Alexandra Pollard), Chris Gartin (Scott), Tandy Cronyn (Meg), Richard Masur (Norm Denton), Ed Begley Jr. (Otis), Luis Avalos (Mr. Riley), Andre Rosey Brown (Security Guard), Charles Champion (Larry Freeman), Ellen Crawford (Rita), Mary Pat Gleason (Receptionist), Jeanine Jackson (Mrs. Oberg), Jean Kasem (Sensuous Witch), Michael Mitz (Ben Hodgkins)

Writer: Robert Zeschin

Director: Larry Elikann

Grace goes to live with her daughter and son-in-law where, after reading a story out loud on public access television, a large company offers her a television series of her own.

Jessica Tandy made this TV movie in her early Eighties, shortly after winning an Oscar for **Driving Miss Daisy**. By 1991 she'd had a long and distinguished career on stage and film, and then, very late in the day, she starred as Grace McQueen in this Christmas film. It's a sweet and gentle tale about the power of storytelling.

Grace is moving in with her daughter and son-in-law, into their smart upstate New York home, leaving behind everything of her own but a few small boxes of possessions. She is surrendering herself to a new life of ease. Her expression of quickly-hidden dismay when confronted with her saccharine pink bedroom is a delight. We know straight away that she won't settle easily for the life her daughter has planned for her. She balks at their sterile modern lives and their meagre diets. There is something so pinched and puritanical about these middle aged prigs she's living with.

Grace dons a smart outfit and puts herself right back on the job market, determined to be of use to someone. No one will have her, however. She can't even read to children in schools or hospitals because their insurance won't cover it. She has a brief moment of existential crisis – what is her role in the world if she can't be of help to anyone, or show anyone she cares?

She remembers reading fairy tales to her daughter. Always the thing she was best at and, when she randomly happens upon public access TV, it's this particular gift that she thinks of first. Seeing ordinary people with their own half hour TV programs sets her mind racing and soon she's decided to become the Story Lady, and to take to the airwaves.

Of course, everyone falls in love with her. She sits in a rocking chair and, at first stumblingly, then with long-practised confidence, she reads Hans Christian Andersen stories. All across Manhattan folk start tuning into her endearingly amateurish show. One of her loyalest fans is the neglected daughter of an advertising executive. She swaps VHS tapes of Grace telling stories with her friends. Quite quickly, it seems, there is a black market in this stuff.

The Story Lady is helped by a young cameraman at the public access station.　Scott is quickly entranced by her talent, emerging from his bored cynicism within moments of recording her first show. He's a film graduate, thoroughly aware that he's frittering away his time in this dump; broadcasting shows about psychic witches and gay aerobics. The slightly shonky world of the TV station is deliciously presented: the wise-cracking receptionist, the bears and snakes and ventriloquist dolls. Jessica Tandy's polite incredulity when she first visits and encounters the Nineties in the raw is marvellous.

It's a film about letting yourself be enchanted: about learning all over again what enchantment means. Stories and love can melt the most frozen of hearts and it's never too late to put things right. These are sentiments all too common in TV movies of this kind, but here, somehow, it all seems fresh and urgent. We really want Grace to find a new place in the world, and we want the little girl, Alexandra, to drag her mother's attention back from her all-absorbing career.

The characters are twined together into the old, old story, when the corporate world becomes aware of Grace's show, and lures her into the big time. Alex's mother Julie's advertising company gets its clutches on Grace and she's drawn into a world of greed and compromise. Grace dotes on Alex, who clearly needs some affection, and all the while Julie's firm is primping and packaging the Story Lady. They want to fix her teeth, dress her up as a fairy tale character, give her dreadful, commercialised nonsense to read out on the air.

It's a Mary Poppins story, though, so, rather than Grace being utterly subsumed and defeated by the corporate world, we see her subtly undermine and defeat it. By the end of the movie she changes everyone's lives for the better, though there are some uncomfortable and heart-rending scenes on the way. (Julie missing her daughter's performance in – what else? – **A Christmas Carol.**)

It's a TV movie. It was probably made quite quickly, alongside a whole lot of other similar movies. It was meant to be a heart-warming couple of hours, nothing more. Just part of the moving wallpaper of daytime TV. Not very different to the hundreds of TV movies made over the years for the festive period. Just another tale in which people are reminded of quasi-Christian values of love and understanding.

I think there's something special about **The Story Lady**, though. I think it's to do with the quality of Jessica Tandy's performance, and the way she brings out the best in everyone she shares moments with. But it's also to do with the film's insistence on a belief in stories, and how the teller must always stick to the truth of their tale – and the warning always to watch out for the wolves in corporate suits.

Also, Scott the young producer in the checked shirt? Who turns up with his 'room mate' at the end? He's hot.

This Morning

Episode Title: This Morning

Channel: Granada

Original UK Transmission Date: 11 December 2006

Regular Cast: Fern Britton (Presenter), Phillip Schofield (Presenter)

Guest Cast: Ben Mills (Himself), Girls Aloud (Themselves), Stephen Merchant (Himself)

I remember these editions of **This Morning** being cosy and friendly.

I've always had a fondness for cheap, throwaway daytime telly. I love anything broadcast live because of the possibility of seeing something go disastrously wrong.

ITV's magazine show **This Morning** has always been a favourite because when it first began I was a student, and became addicted quite easily to its endless chatter and nonsense.

I taped a few shows in the days leading up to Christmas 2006. I was like someone bottling fruit and making jam. I was preserving some kind of festive essence like fizzy wine in old bottles. I was burning an hour or two of yuletide chat onto a disc.

Rewatching it all these years later is rather odd. That jolly presenter, who I remember so warmly, munching her way through homemade mince pies and laughing so spontaneously – doesn't she seem a little bit insincere now? And isn't she a bit patronising when she talks straight into the camera, addressing us at home? There's something slightly schoolmarmish about the way she gently commands our attention. I feel like I'm lying on the sofa, pulling a sickie from school, and she's the teacher who's come round in person to check my temperature and give me homework.

Amazing, isn't it, how time moves on and TV dates so badly? The years are ruthless. Here they are, discussing the **X Factor** semi-final of 2006, broadcast the previous Saturday night. They interview the young man who was cast out[5]. He's grinning, affable, clearly in shellshock. His feet haven't touched the ground. He looks dazzled and disappointed at the same time. He was what they describe as a 'rocker' and he didn't really fit in with the show's poppy format. It was amazing he even got as far

---

[5] Ben Mills was voted out of the third series of X Factor on 9 December, having chosen to sing the Bryan Adams' power ballad '(Everything I Do) I Do It For You' and the U2 track, 'I Still Haven't Found What I'm Looking For'.

as the semi-final and he clearly knows it. His hair is long and freshly blow-dried. He explains his feelings to do with his ejection from the show and maybe how he should have lightened up and been less of a 'rocker.' He dearly wishes he was going to be in the forthcoming final, performing a Christmas song of his own choice.

Then – and this is the truly cruel thing about TV from the archive – this young man talks about his hopes for the future. They ask him about what the new year will bring. Has he stardom ahead in the future as a 'rocker'? He says he has written lots of songs and he has ideas about the people he would like to work with. All he wants is the chance to record his own album.

The presenters coo over him encouragingly and they all wonder about what the future might bring.

Victoria Wood's All-Day Breakfast

Episode Title: Victoria Wood's All-Day Breakfast

Channel: BBC1

Original UK Transmission Date: 25 December 1992

Regular Cast: Victoria Wood (Various), Julie Walters (Various), Celia Imrie (Various), Susie Blake (Various), Duncan Preston (Various)

Guest Cast: Alan Rickman (Himself)

Writer: Victoria Wood

Director: Geoff Posner

*A spoof of morning magazine/chat shows like **This Morning**, presented by Victoria Wood and Duncan Preston, with sketches, exercises and adverts.*

I do love the Nineties – increasingly so. It was the age of irony and daring to experiment; of saying the unsayable and believing that nothing was sacred. Recent years haven't been quite so much fun. Victoria Wood stopped making comedy sketch shows and, if she created a Christmas special in the twenty-first century at all, they tended to be hard-hitting dramas about classical musicians with Alzheimers. (Not quite as much fun.)

Back in the early Nineties the blessed Victoria gave us an extended version of one of her **As Seen on TV** shows from the Eighties. She reunited her core cast of players and set about the serious business of ruthlessly sending up Nineties TV. Things had moved on in the intervening years and Wood had spent some time at home, immersing herself in the relatively new phenomenon of daytime TV. It was still in its infancy and gloriously, mind-bogglingly bad. I was a student then and we loved it all – the magazine shows, the chat shows, the let's-have-a-rowdy-argument shows.

The framing device here is a parody of ITV's **This Morning** with Victoria Wood and Duncan Preston parodying smug husband and wife team, Richard and Judy, who were then having a massive success with their show, casually chatting with a parade of stars and guests and experts in everything and nothing. They were old TV pros and utterly comfortable in front of the camera, which is great, but deadly dangerous also, as their complacency allowed them to come out with utter gibberish in a thoroughly convincing way. Their casual ease at cocking things up and their wince-inducing unguarded asides are sent up brutally by Wood in these sketches. She captures the jarring tone shifts in awkward segues between items and the hollow solemnity of TV presenters is skewered for all time.

Fascist fitness instructors, daft adverts, vacuous celebrity interviews, hard-hitting investigations: they're all taken apart before our very eyes. We are told that, basically, most TV is just glossy rubbish presented by idiots in new clothes on uncomfortable furniture, looking worriedly into the wrong camera.

There's also 'The Mall', a spoof soap which updates Wood's classic 'Acorn Antiques' and sets it in one of those Nineties cathedrals – the out-of-town shopping mall. This lovingly-made parody comes in mini-episodes sprinkled throughout the show and it features just a tad more camp innuendo than usual, and is all the more delightful for it. It's all a bit 'Que sera de brouhaha.'

Wogan

Episode Title: Christmas with the Carringtons

Channel: BBC1

Original UK Transmission Date: 25 December 1985

Regular Cast: Terry Wogan (Host)

Guest Cast: John Forsyth (Himself), Linda Evans (Herself), Kate O'Mara (Herself), Catherine Oxenberg (Herself), John James (Himself), Gordon Thomson (Himself), Michael Praed (Himself), Michael Nader (Himself), Pamela Bellwood (Herself), Jack Coleman (Himself), Diahann Carroll (Herself), Joseph Knowland (The Butler)

Director: Charles Miller

Producer: Jon Plowman

Terry flies out to Denver for Christmas at the Carrington mansion.

It's strange to remember how popular slick and vapid soaps such as **Dynasty** and **Dallas** once were. Looked back at now they have little to recommend them, apart from the more outrageous moments of camp, all of which are usually nicked from old Bette Davis or Joan Crawford movies. These shows are so bogged down in turgid story-telling that it's only possible to enjoy them in a rewatch by dipping in for a little while. It's like being dunked in warm, flat champagne.

Here in Christmas 1985 the BBC sends Terry Wogan to the location of the Carrington mansion, which seems unfeasibly sun-drenched. I can remember how glowing and golden the US as we saw it through soap operas seemed in our grey British winters. Terry spends a whole show on Christmas night on their home turf, talking to the actors from **Dynasty**. They had obviously gained such a level of cultural importance that it didn't even seem weird that this was something we would want to see. As jovial Terry pokes around the rather boring studio set of La Mirage and cosies up to the actors, I imagine we were all agog.

They're all here. Except Joan Collins, the ostensible star of the show. She's having nothing to do with this farrago. Quite a shrewd move, I think, since the programme is actually crushingly dull. Terry does his best to poke fun and be silly with them, as he sits alongside Jeff and Claudia, Adam, Kystle, Blake et al, but it never quite works out. No one is in a very festive mood. He gives them joke presents of Wogan mugs and T-shirts, and they pretend to be delighted. They talk in desultory terms about the show they're starring in. Catherine Oxenberg – with an absurdly posh English accent – comes up with the best line, describing the show as a mixture of 'Turmoil, bitching and incest.' Terry tells her she's talking just the kind of language we all long to hear on Christmas night TV.

133

The way he drifts from table to table in this empty, silent, fake hotel, it's rather like he's stranded in some remote airport lounge, with a bunch of half-drunk actors, who aren't quite sure if they're supposed to be playing themselves or not.

Kate O'Mara had only recently joined the cast, and she is cringing at the whole thing, worrying about how she'll be thought of by the people back at home, and making a plea for the very idea of escapist fantasy.

'Does one really want reality, Terry?' she asks, toying with her glass.

He responds, 'Is that the first drink you've had, dear?'

Epilogue

It was an extremely quiet Christmas. Bernard Socks sat with me, watching all these shows over again. The Christmas food we'd bought went into the freezer. I jammed it all in, tight as a jigsaw, and lived off Wendy's pies. I'd bought a whole box of festive-flavoured pies from our friend Wendy, who'd started a pie-making business that winter. So I just ate pies and watched old telly, and each day I called a taxi to take me to the hospital.

The taxi drivers were great. They didn't charge me double, even on Christmas Day or New Year's Eve. They were all Muslims and they told me with great glee that only Muslims were driving taxis through Christmas and charging decent prices: everyone else was a rip-off.

The hospital was over-warm and busy. Everyone was in Santa-themed jumpers and being cheerful. Jeremy was on the strongest painkillers they could give him for days. The worst of the things he went through was when I wasn't there. On Christmas night he was stuck with rather callous relief nurses who just looked at him and shrugged when he begged for stronger painkillers. They hadn't been authorised to give any and they weren't going to phone anyone for permission. They just left him lying on the floor.

But others treated him well. There was a very brisk, very gay Spanish nurse who made sure he went to the right department and kept a beady, clever eye on him. He was appalled at the lax attention paid to him for the first couple of days.

Luckily he didn't need surgery to sort out the blockage in his system. The spasms and the waves of pain slowly went away.

There were strange, dramatic moments, such as when a young man in the next bed was practically dying overnight of a ruptured bowel. Somehow he was allowed to have his minister and what seemed like his entire church congregation visit him in the wee small hours. They prayed and sobbed over him. They howled and performed an exorcism as if his intestines were inhabited by demons. Jeremy said it was extremely frightening and disturbing.

He also witnessed a punch-up in the X-Ray department.

There was allsorts going on at the Manchester infirmary that Christmas.

We hung a glittery Bambi above his bed. A present from our friend in Wales, Rosie, and that was his Christmas decoration: this prancing, grinning deer.

I came each day with fresh pyjamas and his iPad, loaded up with Christmas TV shows. He wasn't very impressed with anything telly had to offer that year, and neither was I, really.

They let him out on New Year's Eve – too early, really. He still wasn't strong enough. But he'd been in for a week, and if he stayed one more night he'd be stuck there four days, till after the bank holiday weekend. We called a taxi, and waited for him to be discharged and to be given his medications.

And eventually, in the early hours we were home. He was still shouting out in pain, but he was home. Bernard Socks was delirious with pleasure.

It took him several days to be able to come downstairs.

We held an impromptu Christmas early in January.

Out came the presents and the turkey and the party food. Out came the discs of old telly. Putting on **The Good Life**, **The Box of Delights**, **Cagney and Lacey**, **The Real Christmas Show**, **K9**

and Company, **Crossroads**... they were an essential part of summoning up the right atmosphere for creating a belated holiday, just as the rest of the country was emerging from their own.

It reminded me of that old urban legend about the cat-worshipping club. Do you know it?

A small cult of some kind used to get together to do unspeakable rites, quite regularly. As soon as they started chanting and stuff, the cat would go wild with excitement, dashing about, screeching, demanding attention.

They ended up having to tie it down to the bed. Which seems cruel and unnecessary, but they were a cult, weren't they? They were probably all crackers. Anyway, it worked, and the cat, once tied down to the mattress, kept quiet and stopped interrupting.

Anyway, time went on, and it all became part of the ritual.

And eventually, people forgot what it was they were chanting and worshipping for. They just carried things out by rote. They even lost track of what unspeakable rites they were supposed to be performing. As people in the cult came and went and younger people took over, the emphasis shifted.

Now, they met up and did the most important part first. They tied the excitable cat to the bed. And then they simply worshipped the cat.

Gradually, by degrees, they became the cult who tied cats to beds in order to worship them.

The cats never said anything. They thought humans were crazy anyway, and they quite liked the attention, even if it meant being tied up for a while.

That's how it seems to me. Telly – especially Christmas telly – is a cat tied to a mattress with a cult standing round it, worshipping and chanting and going through the motions of an old ritual. Hoping that the whole thing will bring back the feelings of the way it used to be.

The Christmas we created in early January made us realise that, actually, it can be Christmas any day you want it to be.

It's a thing you summon up between you – a shared illusion – rather than something that happens to a waiting world.

You can bring the feeling on any time you want. It's preserved in a scent. Or an old story, a photograph, or a song. Christmas can even be on an old videotape.

It can be kept magically preserved in a box of discs.

BIBLIOGRAPHY

Television

Blankety Blank. BBC, 1979-1990, 1997-2002, 2016.

    Christmas, 1981

The Box of Delights. BBC, 1984.

Cagney and Lacey. CBS, 1981-88.

    I'll be Home for Christmas, 1983

Camp Christmas. Channel 4. 1993.

Christmas Spirits. Granada. 1981

Doctor Who. BBC, 1963-.

    The Christmas Invasion, 2005.

Emu's World. ITV. 1982-1984.

    Emu's World at Christmas, 1983.

Fame. MGM Television, 1982-87.

    All I Want for Christmas, 1986.

Frasier. Paramount Television, 1993-2004.

    Perspectives on Christmas, 1998.

The Good Life. BBC, 1975-78.

    Silly, but it's Fun, 1977.

K9 and Company. BBC, 1981

    A Girl's Best Friend, 1981.

Larry Grayson's Generation Game. BBC, 1978-82.

The Morecambe and Wise Show. BBC, 1968-77.

Christmas Show, 1975.

Omnibus. BBC, 1967-2003.

Whistle and I'll Come to You, 1968.

Sherlock Holmes. BBC, 1964-68.

The Blue Carbuncle. 1968.

The Real Christmas Show. Channel 4, 1996.

This Morning. Granada, 1988-.

Victoria Wood's All Day Breakfast. BBC, 1992.

Wogan. BBC, 1982-1993.

Film

Reed, Bill and   Ernie Schmidt, dir, *He Man and She-Ra: A Christmas Special*, Filmation, 1985.

Harris, Peter, dir, *A Muppet Family Christmas*, Jim Henson Company, 1987.

Jackson, Dianne, dir, *The Snowman,* TVC London, 1982.

Elikann, Larry, dir, *The Story Lady,*. NBC Productions, 1991.

BIOGRAPHY

Paul Magrs lives and writes in Manchester. In a twenty-odd year writing career he has published novels in every genre from Literary to Gothic Mystery to Science Fiction. His most recent books **are The Martian Girl** (Firefly Press) and **Fellowship of Ink** (Snowbooks.)

He has taught Creative Writing at both the University of East Anglia and Manchester Metropolitan University, and now writes full time.